Grilling
MAESTROS

FUNDING PROVIDED BY:

Grilling
MAESTROS

Produced by Marjorie Poore Productions

Photographs by Alec Fatalevich

Table of Contents

Introduction

MAESTRO—master, creator, artisan, craftsman—Marcel Desaulniers, Chris Schlesinger and Fritz Sonnenschmidt are all of these and more. Featured in the public television series and book *Grilling Maestros,* three of the best chefs in the country add new and exciting dimensions to the art form of cooking by applying their considerable know-how to the art of grilling. We are fortunate to have these three masters share their diverse recipes, techniques and knowledge with us. The unusual blending of ingredients, combined with the transformation of food by fire, smoke and wood, creates new, yet beloved flavors and smells as if by magic.

Guests from all over the world have made Williamsburg, Virginia their destination for keeping in touch with history and for dining at Marcel Desaulniers' Trellis Restaurant. Already in the early 80's The Trellis Restaurant under chef Desaulniers became internationally known for being among the first culinary establishments to offer seasonal menus with fresh ingredients. With his landmark *Death by Chocolate* and many other cookbooks, our grilling maestro Marcel Desaulniers established himself nationwide as the "king of chocolate" and popular resource for serious home-chefs. Grilling has always been important at The Trellis Restaurant, and we are delighted that Chef Desaulniers has shared his elegant, easy-to-prepare grilling recipes with us.

Maestro Chris Schlesinger did for grilling in the 80's what Julia Child did for French cooking in the 70's. Many of us grew up on grilled hamburgers, hot dogs and an occasional steak or chicken, often burned beyond recognition. We would probably still be eating those barbecue staples if it weren't for

Chris, chef/owner of the wildly popular East Coast Grill in Cambridge and the Back Eddy restaurant in Westport, Massachusetts, where the food is as sensational as the setting. Chris' books *Thrill of the Grill* and *License to Grill* opened our eyes to the endless combinations of ingredients and the great variety of foods, which can be used to prepare great meals by grilling. A true understanding of fire (the grill chef's best friend or worst enemy) is essential in teaching any cook how to approach a grill with confidence and passion.

Fritz Sonnenschmidt, C.M.C., our third grilling maestro, has a heart warm enough to light any grill, as the many culinary students once and now under his tutelage will readily confirm. Students from all over the country flock to the prestigious Culinary Institute of America, just for a chance to be taught by Fritz, Culinary Dean of that institution. Naturally, his expertise extends to all areas of cooking, but those who know him well are aware of his special passion for grilling. In *Grilling Maestros* Fritz demonstrates with his usual sense of humor why heat control, flavor pairing and doneness are essential for great cooking on the grill.

The pleasures of outdoor cooking will be broadened immensely if you let our grilling maestros show you how to do it.   *—Marjorie Poore*

Beginnings and Endings

All-Purpose Ash-Roasted Garlic

Chris Schlesinger | Reprinted from *License to Grill*, William Morrow and Company

4 large heads garlic, loose peel rubbed off
¼ cup olive oil
Salt and freshly ground black pepper to taste

CUT ABOUT ¼ inch from the top of the garlic heads. Place the garlic heads in the center of a sheet of heavy-duty aluminum foil about 1 foot long. Pour the oil over the garlic and sprinkle with salt and pepper to taste, then cover with a second sheet of foil and roll the edges of the two sheets together on all sides, closing the pack. Place the pack in the center of another 1-foot length of foil and fold this length up around the pack.

LAY THE PACKET in the dying embers of a medium to low fire and pile coals up on all sides. Cook the garlic for 35 minutes, moving it around occasionally to keep it in contact with the glowing coals. Remove the pack from the coals and unroll the foil. Cool. ◉

Grilled Garlic

Fritz Sonnenschmidt

4 heads fresh garlic, loose peel rubbed off
Olive oil

CUT ABOUT ¼ inch from the top of the garlic heads. Brush the heads with the olive oil and place on a grill over medium-high heat. Cover the grill and cook for 30 to 40 minutes, or until the garlic is golden brown and soft to the touch. Cool. ◉

Chris roasts garlic using his "hobo pack" technique: He wraps whole heads of garlic tightly with heavy-duty foil and plunges them right into the ashes of a dying fire. Fritz, on the other hand, tosses garlic heads directly onto the grill and cooks them until soft and golden brown. The result of both recipes is a sweet, nutty, mellow garlic pulp with just a hint of smokiness. Decide for yourself which method you prefer.

SERVES 4

Grilled Hungarian Peppers

Fritz Sonnenschmidt

A trio of sweet bell peppers are grilled, then pickled in a solution of vinegar, sugar, herbs, and spices. This makes an intriguing accompaniment for sliced bread.

SERVES 4 TO 6

3 yellow bell peppers

3 red bell peppers

3 green bell peppers

1 pound shallots

1 pint cider vinegar

2 teaspoons dried oregano

2 bay leaves

1 ½ pounds sugar

Salt and freshly ground black pepper to taste

4 heads Grilled Garlic, page 9

California sourdough bread for an accompaniment

PREHEAT THE GRILL to high heat.

CUT THE PEPPERS in half, remove the stems and seeds, and cut into quarters.

PEEL THE SHALLOTS and cut each into 3 to 4 disks.

SPRAY THE VEGETABLES with olive oil cooking spray and place on the grill. Grill for 5 minutes on each side.

TRANSFER THE VEGETABLES to a large skillet and add the vinegar, oregano, bay leaves, sugar, salt and pepper. Squeeze the grilled garlic into the skillet and bring the mixture to a boil over high heat. Reduce the heat to low and simmer for 3 to 4 minutes. Cool and refrigerate.

SERVE WITH THIN SLICES of California sourdough bread. ◉

Grilled Chicken Wings

Fritz Sonnenschmidt | Recipe Courtesy of the Weber-Stephen Products Co.

Always popular at parties, grilled chicken wings with an Asian twist will win raves. Provide lots of napkins for your guests.

SERVES 6

18 whole chicken wings (about 4 pounds)

2 tablespoons reduced-sodium soy sauce

2 tablespoons dry sherry

2 tablespoons vegetable oil

1 tablespoon toasted sesame oil

2 to 3 drops hot pepper sauce

Asian Dipping Sauce, follows

Chinese cabbage leaves (optional)

CUT OFF AND DISCARD the small wing tips from the chicken wings. Cut each wing at the joint to make 2 sections.

IN A SMALL BOWL, combine the soy sauce, sherry, vegetable oil, sesame oil, and hot sauce. Place the chicken wing pieces in a large plastic resealable bag. Pour the marinade over the chicken; close the bag and refrigerate for 1 hour.

REMOVE THE CHICKEN WINGS from the marinade. Place the chicken wings in the center of the grill's cooking grate. Grill over medium–low heat for 15 minutes or until tender, turning once halfway through the grilling time.

BRUSH ABOUT ½ cup of the Asian Dipping Sauce on the chicken wing pieces. Continue grilling for 2 to 3 minutes, turning once halfway through the grilling time. Remove the chicken wings from the grill and arrange on a platter with Chinese cabbage leaves, if desired. Serve with the remaining Asian Dipping Sauce on the side. ◉

Asian Dipping Sauce

3 tablespoons vegetable oil

1 teaspoon minced fresh ginger

1 scallion, chopped

½ cup chicken broth

3 tablespoons dark soy sauce

2 tablespoons packed brown sugar

1 teaspoon chili powder

¼ teaspoon red pepper flakes

3 teaspoons cornstarch

1 tablespoon dry sherry

IN A SMALL SAUCEPAN, heat the oil over medium heat. Add the ginger and scallion and cook for 1 minute, or until browned. Add the chicken broth, soy sauce, brown sugar, chili powder, and red pepper. Bring to a boil. Dissolve the cornstarch in the sherry; add gradually to the soy sauce mixture, stirring constantly until slightly thickened. Serve warm. ◉

Barbecued Clams in Their Shells

Chris Schlesinger | Reprinted from *License to Grill*, William Morrow and Company

½ cup unsalted butter

1 tablespoon minced garlic

2 tablespoons fresh lemon juice (about ½ lemon)

¼ cup Tabasco sauce

¼ cup Worcestershire sauce

Salt and freshly ground black pepper to taste

4 dozen clams of your choice, washed well

¼ cup roughly chopped fresh parsley

2 lemons, quartered

BUILD A MEDIUM-HOT charcoal fire in the grill.

IN A SHALLOW BAKING PAN, combine the butter and garlic and place at the edge of the fire to melt the butter. When the butter has melted, add the lemon juice, Tabasco, Worcestershire, and salt and pepper to taste and stir everything together.

PLACE THE CLAMS on the grill, directly over the fire, and cook for 2 to 3 minutes. At this point you can pull them off and open them with a clam knife, or you can leave them on for another 1 to 2 minutes until they open themselves. Discard any that do not open.

SPRINKLE THE CLAMS with the parsley, douse with the butter sauce, and serve in their shells, with the lemon quarters for spritzing. ◉

Heating fresh oysters on the grill causes their shells to pop open and makes them easy to pry apart. They are infused with charcoal flavor, which is accented by a spicy butter sauce. You can use the same cooking technique and sauce to prepare fresh oysters or mussels.

SERVES 4 TO 8

Grilled Chicken Thighs with Peach, Black Olive, and Red Onion Relish

Chris Schlesinger | Reprinted from *The Thrill of the Grill*, William Morrow and Company

Sweet ripe peaches and briny kalamata olives pair surprisingly well in a relish to top grilled chicken thighs. The flavor of chicken thighs is a little deeper and richer than chicken breasts and stands up well to the assertive flavors of the relish. You can substitute other fresh black olives for the kalamatas, but do not use canned olives.

SERVES 8

3 ripe peaches

½ cup fresh black kalamata olives

1 small red onion, diced small

1 roasted red bell pepper, diced small

4 tablespoons extra-virgin olive oil

2 tablespoons balsamic vinegar

1 teaspoon minced garlic

1 tablespoon fresh thyme leaves

Salt and freshly ground black pepper to taste

4 tablespoons lemon juice (about 1 lemon)

8 chicken thighs

PIT THE PEACHES and cut them into pieces about the size of sugar cubes. Pit the olives and cut them in half.

COMBINE THE PEACHES, olives, onion, and red pepper in a mixing bowl.

ADD THE OLIVE OIL, vinegar, garlic, and thyme, and toss lightly. Add the salt and pepper to taste.

COVER THE MIXTURE and allow it to stand at room temperature for at least 1 hour. It will keep, covered in the refrigerator, for up to 3 days.

JUST BEFORE SERVING, add the lemon juice and mix lightly.

SEASON THE CHICKEN thighs with salt and pepper to taste. Grill the chicken thighs skin-side down over medium-low heat, for 8 to 10 minutes, or until the skin is crispy. Flip them over and cook for an additional 4 to 6 minutes. To check for doneness: Make an incision close to the bone and look for redness, which you don't want. Serve them warm or cold with the peach relish. ◉

Seared Sirloin, Sushi-Style

Chris Schlesinger | Reprinted from *The Thrill of the Grill*, William Morrow and Company

Spice Rub

1 tablespoon freshly cracked white pepper

1 tablespoon freshly cracked black pepper

1 tablespoon kosher salt

1 tablespoon five-spice powder

1 tablespoon paprika

1 teaspoon powdered ginger

One 16- to 20-ounce sirloin steak, 2 inches thick, trimmed of all the fat
  (let your butcher prepare it)

½ cup soy sauce

6 ounces pickled ginger

4 tablespoons wasabi powder, mixed thoroughly with 4 tablespoons water

MAKE THE SPICE RUB: Mix the white and black peppers, salt, five spice powder, paprika, and ginger, and rub the steak on all sides with the spice mixture. Allow it to stand, uncovered, at room temperature for 1 hour.

OVER A VERY HOT FIRE, heavily sear the steak on all its surfaces, 2 minutes per surface. (You will have four surfaces on a steak this thick: top, bottom, and two sides.) You are looking for a well-browned, thoroughly seared surface, but since you want the heat to penetrate only the outer layer of the meat, you must be sure to do it at a very high heat.

REMOVE THE MEAT from the grill and allow it to cool for at least 20 minutes before serving. If you want, you can refrigerate it, covered, for up to 2 days, and bring it out an hour before serving to remove the chill.

SLICE THE MEAT paper-thin across the grain and arrange it on a platter with small dishes of soy sauce, ginger, and wasabi. ◉

Fans of Italian carpaccio will devour this Japanese interpretation. Treat this as you would sushi, using the soy sauce, wasabi and pickled ginger as condiments. Look for these ingredients and the five-spice powder in an Asian market or specialty food store.

SERVES 4

Grilled Peaches with Blue Cheese and Sweet Balsamic Glaze

Chris Schlesinger | Reprinted from *Big Flavors of the Hot Sun*, William Morrow and Company

Fruit and cheese are a classic combination anytime you serve them, whether as a prelude to a meal or a finale. Chris recommends making a double batch of the pepper-infused balsamic glaze, as it is wonderful brushed on chicken or fish just before removing them from the grill.

SERVES 4 AS APPETIZER OR DESSERT

1 cup good-quality balsamic vinegar

2 tablespoons sugar

1 tablespoon freshly ground black pepper

3 peaches, halved and pitted

2 tablespoons virgin olive oil (approximately)

4 ounces blue cheese of your choice, crumbled

IN A SMALL SAUCEPAN, combine the vinegar, sugar, and pepper and bring to a boil. Reduce the heat to low and simmer, stirring occasionally, for 45 minutes to 1 hour, or until reduced in volume by about two-thirds. At this point, the glaze should be thick enough to coat the back of a spoon.

RUB THE PEACH halves with olive oil and grill over medium to medium-low heat until just slightly charred, 8 to 10 minutes. Brush the tops with the glaze and grill for another 2 to 3 minutes, or until the glaze begins to caramelize slightly.

REMOVE THE PEACHES from the grill, brush on another layer of glaze, and cut into thick slices. Place the slices on individual plates, crumble the cheese over them, and serve. ◉

Grilled Banana Splits

Chris Schlesinger | Reprinted from *Big Flavors of the Hot Sun*, William Morrow and Company

A new twist on banana splits features molasses-glazed bananas and a liqueur-spiked raspberry sauce. Consider these banana splits for grown-ups. You can substitute mangos, strawberries, or any other sweet fruit for the raspberries in the sauce.

SERVES 4

¼ cup lime juice (about 2 limes)

2 tablespoons molasses

4 ripe bananas, unpeeled, halved lengthwise

Raspberry Sauce

1 pint fresh raspberries, halved (you may substitute frozen)

2 tablespoons sugar

2 tablespoons Triple Sec or rum

1 pint ice cream of your choice

½ cup chopped pecans or other nuts

1 cup heavy cream, whipped

IN A SMALL BOWL, combine the lime juice and molasses and mix well.

PLACE THE BANANA halves on the grill, cut-sides down, over medium heat and grill for about 4 minutes, or until just golden. Flip the bananas over, paint the cut sides with the lime-molasses glaze, and grill, glazed-sides up, for an additional 2 minutes. Remove from the grill.

WHILE THE BANANAS are cooking, make the Raspberry Sauce: Puree the raspberries, sugar, and Triple Sec or rum in a blender or food processor until well blended.

SERVE THE BANANAS topped with ice cream, Raspberry Sauce, nuts, and whipped cream. ◉

Grilled Bananas and Pineapple with Rum-Molasses Glaze

Chris Schlesinger | Reprinted from *License to Grill*, William Morrow and Company

¼ *cup dark rum*

¼ *cup molasses*

¼ *cup unsalted butter*

2 tablespoons fresh lime juice (about 1 lime)

4 bananas, unpeeled, halved lengthwise

½ *ripe pineapple, unpeeled, cut into 4 slices about* ½*-inch thick*

3 tablespoons vegetable oil

1 pint ice cream of your choice

IN A SMALL SAUCEPAN, combine the rum, molasses, butter, and lime juice. Cook over medium heat, stirring frequently, until the butter is melted and the ingredients are well blended. Remove from the heat.

RUB THE BANANA halves and pineapple slices lightly with the oil. Place on the grill, with the bananas cut-side down, and grill over medium heat for about 2 minutes, or until the bananas are just golden and the pineapple slices have acquired light grill marks. Flip the fruit over, paint with the rum-molasses glaze, and grill for an additional 1 minute. Remove from the grill.

SERVE EACH PERSON 2 banana halves and a slice of pineapple (peeled if you want to make it easy for your guests), topped with a scoop of ice cream. If there is leftover glaze, drizzle it over the ice cream. ◉

Leaving the peel on the bananas and pineapple helps the fruit to remain whole while grilling. You can remove the peels just before serving, or let your guests do it themselves.

SERVES 4

Grilled Fruit Medley

Fritz Sonnenschmidt

Marinade

1 cup fresh orange juice

½ cup balsamic vinegar

½ cup sugar

½ cup butter, melted

¼ cup brandy

1 pear, cut into quarters and core removed

1 orange, cut into ¼-inch-thick slices

1 banana, peeled and cut in half

1 peach, pitted and cut into quarters

2 apricots, pitted and cut in half

Sliced French bread (optional)

Vanilla ice cream (optional)

IN A LARGE SHALLOW BOWL, combine the marinade ingredients. Add the fruit and carefully toss to coat the fruit with the marinade. Let the fruit stand in the marinade for 20 minutes.

DRAIN THE FRUIT and transfer the marinade to a small saucepan. Place the fruit on a grill over medium–high heat and grill for 1 to 2 minutes per side. While the fruit is grilling, bring the marinade to a boil and remove from the heat.

DIVIDE THE GRILLED FRUIT mixture among 6 dessert bowls and pour the hot marinade mixture into the bowl as a sauce. Serve warm with French bread or ice cream, if desired. ◉

You can use almost any type of firm fruit for this recipe, such as citrus fruit, stone fruit, and pineapple. Take a trip to the farmstand and collect what's available in season. Fresh berries, such as blueberries, make a delightful garnish.

SERVES 4 TO 6

Bananas Calypso

Fritz Sonnenschmidt | Recipe Courtesy of the Weber-Stephen Products Co.

Impress your guests with this flaming concoction of rum-spiked bananas over ice cream. For another tropical treat, you can substitute 1-inch-thick semifirm peeled mango slices for bananas (2 mangos).

SERVES 4

⅓ cup sugar

¼ cup unsalted butter, melted

2 tablespoons lime juice (about 1 lime)

½ to 1 teaspoon ground cinnamon

4 firm, ripe bananas (about 1 pound), peeled

⅓ cup dark rum

4 scoops vanilla ice cream

IN A SMALL BOWL, combine the sugar, melted butter, lime juice, and cinnamon. Brush the bananas with about ¼ cup of the butter mixture. Place the bananas on the center of the cooking grate. Grill over medium–low heat for 2 to 4 minutes, turning once halfway through grilling time. Slice the grilled bananas and place the slices in a flameproof dish.

POUR THE REMAINING butter mixture over the bananas. Place the dish on the center of the grill's cooking grate and cook for 5 minutes. Remove the dish from the grill.

QUICKLY POUR THE RUM over the bananas. With a long kitchen match, ignite the rum. After the flames die out, serve immediately over ice cream. ◉

Grilled Omelet Soufflé

Fritz Sonnenschmidt

10 eggs, separated

½ teaspoon vanilla extract

3 tablespoons granulated sugar

2 tablespoons flour

1 ½ cups milk

2 tablespoons butter

6 rye bread croutons

6 teaspoons raspberry jam

Confectioners' sugar

1 cup walnuts, toasted

PREHEAT A GAS grill to medium.

IN A BOWL, whip the egg yolks with the vanilla extract until pale yellow in color.

IN ANOTHER BOWL, whip the egg whites with the granulated sugar until stiff peaks form.

ADD ABOUT 2 tablespoons of the egg white mixture to the egg yolk mixture and mix gently. Add the flour and mix gently until combined. Fold the remaining egg white mixture into the egg yolk mixture until combined.

IN A SAUCEPAN, bring the milk and butter just to a boil; remove from the heat.

SPREAD EACH CROUTON with 1 teaspoon of the raspberry jam and arrange the croutons in a greased fireproof dish so that they just fit. Pour the hot milk mixture into the dish. With a large spoon, add the egg mixture.

PLACE THE DISH on the grill over indirect heat and cook for approximately 12 minutes, until the eggs are fully set, but not dry.

SPOON PORTIONS of the omelet soufflé onto warmed dessert plates and sprinkle with confectioners' sugar. Serve immediately with the toasted walnuts. ◉

Here's a unique dessert that can be "baked" on the grill after the entrée is cooked. To make the rye bread croutons, cut stale pieces of rye bread into 3- to 4-inch rounds with a circular cutter. Place them in a 250-degree oven until they are dry and crisp.

SERVES 6

Sides and Salads

Eggplant and Tomato Hobo Pack with Lemon and Garlic

Chris Schlesinger | Reprinted from *License to Grill*, William Morrow and Company

2 lemons, cut into thin rounds

2 small eggplants, cut lengthwise into quarters

4 plum tomatoes, halved

2 heads garlic, halved horizontally

7 large sprigs fresh oregano or rosemary

¼ cup olive oil

Salt and freshly ground black pepper to taste

LAY OUT TWO SHEETS of heavy–duty foil, each about two–feet long, one on top of the other. Place the lemon slices in the center, then put the eggplant quarters on top. Follow with the tomatoes and garlic, add the herbs, drizzle with the olive oil and season with salt and pepper. Lay a third length of heavy–duty foil over the top. Fold the edges of the foil sheets together on all sides, closing the pack, then roll them up until they bump into the food, forming a ridge around its perimeter. Place the pack right–side up in the center of a fourth length of foil and fold the four sides over the top of the packet, one after another.

NOW THE PACKAGE is ready for the coals. The fire should have passed its peak of intensity and be dying down, so that it consists primarily of blowing coals covered with a thin film of gray ash, but very few flickering flames–in other words, you want a medium to low dying fire. Clear a place for the foil packet, leaving a thin layer of coals. Place the packet on the cleared area and heap up coals all around, but not directly on top. Cook, keeping watch and shifting the packet as needed so it is continuously in contact with glowing coals, for 20 to 30 minutes, depending on the intensity of the coals.

REMOVE THE PACKET from the coals, unroll the foil and serve at once. ◉

For one of Chris's favorite cooking methods, "hobo pack cookery," foods are wrapped tightly in aluminum foil and placed right into the charcoal ashes. The secret to success lies in using heavy-duty foil, a large quantity of it, and following Chris's instructions for wrapping.

SERVES 4 TO 6

Spicy Eggplant in Garlic Sauce

Fritz Sonnenschmidt | Recipe Courtesy of the Weber-Stephen Products Co.

The Asian-style sauce that coats the eggplant strips is easy to put together from prepared items found in the international aisle in the supermarket or in any Asian market. A good dose of minced fresh ginger and garlic adds lively flavor.

SERVES 6

1½ pounds eggplant, peeled and cut into 1x1x2-inch strips

1 green bell pepper, cut into 1x2-inch strips

1 red bell pepper, cut into 1x2-inch strips

⅔ cup olive oil

1 teaspoon minced fresh ginger

1 teaspoon minced garlic

½ tablespoon hoisin sauce or hot bean sauce

¼ cup sugar

¼ cup rice vinegar

¼ cup chicken broth

¼ cup light soy sauce

¼ cup dark soy sauce

1 tablespoon toasted sesame oil

2 tablespoons cornstarch

2 tablespoons water

PLACE THE EGGPLANT and pepper strips in large bowl. Pour ⅓ cup of the oil over the strips and toss to coat.

PLACE THE VEGETABLES in the center of the grill's cooking grate over low heat. Grill for 6 to 8 minutes, turning halfway.

MEANWHILE, IN SMALL SAUCEPAN, heat the remaining ⅓ cup oil over medium heat. Add the ginger and garlic and sauté for 1 minute, until brown. Stir in the hoisin sauce. Quickly add the sugar, vinegar, chicken broth, light soy sauce, dark soy sauce, and sesame oil. Bring to a boil.

STIR THE CORNSTARCH into the water until dissolved. Add the cornstarch mixture to the sauce and stir until thickened.

TRANSFER THE GRILLED VEGETABLES to a serving bowl, pour the sauce over the vegetables and toss to coat. Serve immediately. ◉

Grilled Eggplant Rounds with Sweet Chile Sauce

Chris Schlesinger | Reprinted from *License to Grill*, William Morrow and Company

Sweet Chile Sauce

2 tablespoons sesame oil

1 tablespoon minced garlic

1 teaspoon minced fresh ginger

½ cup fresh lime juice (about 3 to 4 limes)

2 tablespoons ketchup

2 tablespoons brown sugar

2 teaspoons minced fresh chile peppers of your choice

2 medium eggplants, cut into rounds about 1-inch thick

¼ cup vegetable oil

Salt and freshly ground black pepper to taste

8 scallions (white and green parts), thinly sliced on the bias

3 tablespoons coriander seeds, toasted if you want, or 1½ tablespoons ground coriander

1 tablespoon red pepper flakes

MAKE THE SAUCE: In a medium saucepan, heat the sesame oil over medium heat until hot, but not smoking. Add the garlic and ginger and sauté, stirring occasionally, for 3 minutes. Add the lime juice, ketchup, brown sugar, and chile peppers and bring to a boil, stirring occasionally. Reduce the heat to low and simmer, stirring once in a while, for 20 minutes, or until the sauce is thick enough to coat the back of a spoon. Remove from the heat and set aside.

PUT THE EGGPLANT rounds into a medium bowl along with the vegetable oil and salt and pepper to taste, and toss to coat. Cook the eggplant on the grill over medium–high heat and cook until browned and soft, about 4 minutes per side. To check for doneness: Cut into the eggplant and check to be sure the interior looks moist. Brush the eggplant on both sides with the chile sauce, leave it on the grill for about 10 seconds, and then remove it from the grill. Sprinkle with the scallions, coriander, and red pepper flakes, and serve warm. ◉

This dish has many flavors—tangy, sweet, spicy, and smoky—which fuse into a delectable glaze to top tender grilled eggplant rounds.

SERVES 4

Grilled Eggplant with Mustard–Miso Sauce

Fritz Sonnenschmidt | Recipe Courtesy of the Weber-Stephen Products Co.

1 medium eggplant, peeled and cut crosswise into 1-inch-thick slices

Vegetable oil

Mustard-Miso Sauce, follows

BRUSH THE EGGPLANT slices with vegetable oil.

PLACE THE EGGPLANT slices on the grill over medium–high heat. Grill for 10 minutes. Turn and grill for 5 minutes.

SPREAD THE TOP of each eggplant slice with Mustard–Miso Sauce and grill for 5 minutes, or until the sauce begins to speckle. Serve immediately. ◉

Miso, or fermented soybean paste, is a staple in Japanese cookery. Here it is combined with Dijon-style mustard, soy sauce, rice wine, and other ingredients for a sweet and spicy coating for silky grilled eggplant.

SERVES 4

Mustard–Miso Sauce

2 tablespoons sesame seeds, toasted

½ cup Dijon-style mustard

1 tablespoon white miso

1 tablespoon mirin (sweet rice wine)

1 tablespoon soy sauce

1 tablespoon sugar

1 teaspoon toasted sesame oil

Hot pepper sauce to taste (optional)

IN A FOOD PROCESSOR fitted with the steel blade, process the sesame seeds until powdery and transfer to a small bowl.

ADD THE MUSTARD, miso, mirin, soy sauce, sugar, sesame oil, and hot pepper sauce, if using, and mix thoroughly. Cover and store in the refrigerator until ready to use. ◉

Summer Vegetable Ratatouille

Marcel Desaulniers

Definitely a dish to make ahead of time, this dish requires four hours to marinate. This is the perfect side dish for a picnic on a sweltering summer day, since it requires no cooking, just a few minutes spent chopping the fresh vegetables and herbs.

SERVES 4

3 tablespoons cider vinegar

1½ tablespoons fresh lemon juice (about ½ lemon)

2 teaspoons Dijon-style mustard

½ teaspoon salt

¼ teaspoon freshly ground black pepper

¾ cup extra-virgin olive oil

½ tablespoon chopped fresh basil

½ teaspoon minced garlic

½ pound zucchini, lightly peeled, cut into ½-inch cubes

½ pound yellow squash, lightly peeled, cut into ½-inch cubes

¼ pound green bell pepper, seeded and cut into ¼-inch pieces

¼ pound red bell pepper, seeded and cut into ¼-inch pieces

¼ pound red onion, cut into ¼-inch pieces

1 medium tomato, peeled, seeded, and chopped

MAKE A VINAIGRETTE by whisking together in a stainless steel bowl the vinegar, lemon juice, mustard, salt, and pepper. Slowly whisk in ¾ cup olive oil in a slow, steady stream until incorporated. Add the basil and garlic, and whisk to combine. Cover the bowl with plastic wrap and set aside at room temperature until needed.

COMBINE THE ZUCCHINI, yellow squash, bell peppers, onion, and tomato in a large stainless steel bowl. Whisk the vinaigrette, then pour over the vegetables. Use a rubber spatula to thoroughly combine. Cover tightly with plastic wrap and refrigerate for at least 4 hours. ◉

Zucchini Gratin

Fritz Sonnenschmidt

3 tablespoons olive oil

1 onion, finely chopped

2 cloves garlic, finely chopped

1 pound tomatoes, peeled, seeded, and coarsely chopped

½ to 1 teaspoon salt

1 teaspoon chopped fresh rosemary

1 teaspoon honey

3 drops hot pepper sauce

½ head romaine lettuce, cut into very thin strips

2 pounds zucchini, cut into 1-inch cubes

8 ounces rye bread, grated

2 ounces sour cream

IN A SKILLET, heat 1 tablespoon of the oil over medium heat. Add the onion and garlic and sauté for 2 minutes.

ADD THE TOMATOES, salt, rosemary, honey, and hot sauce, and cook over low heat for 10 minutes. Add the romaine and mix well.

IN ANOTHER SKILLET, heat the remaining 2 tablespoons olive oil over medium heat and sauté the zucchini until golden brown.

IN A BOWL, mix the rye bread with sour cream.

PLACE THE TOMATO MIXTURE in a casserole, spreading evenly. Top with a layer of zucchini. Spread the zucchini evenly with the sour cream mixture.

COVER THE CASSEROLE and place on a grill over medium–high heat. Cook for 20 minutes, until hot throughout. ◉

The grill does double-duty as an oven to bake this flavorful vegetable casserole. Grated rye bread helps bind the ingredients together and adds a surprising flavor to the dish.

SERVES 4 TO 6

Chilled Spinach with Soy and Ginger

Chris Schlesinger | Reprinted from *The Thrill of the Grill*, William Morrow and Company

A salad in the Japanese-style, this intensely-flavored dish is meant to be served in small portions to accompany simple grilled foods.

SERVES 6

3 tablespoons sesame seeds

2 pounds fresh spinach, stems removed, washed, and dried

3 tablespoons toasted sesame oil

3 tablespoons rice vinegar

4 tablespoons soy sauce

1 tablespoon minced fresh ginger

2 teaspoons sugar

3 dashes Tabasco sauce

Freshly cracked pepper to taste (white is best)

PREHEAT THE OVEN to 350°F. Spread the sesame seeds on a baking sheet in a single layer and bake for 25 minutes, until toasted.

FILL YOUR SINK with about 5 quarts of water and a couple of trays of ice cubes.

IN 3 QUARTS OF BOILING WATER, cook the spinach very briefly, about 15 to 20 seconds. Remove it, drain, and plunge immediately into the ice–water bath. (This is important to stop the cooking and retain the vibrant green color of the spinach.) After 30 seconds or so, drain the spinach again, chop it coarsely, and place it in a large mixing bowl.

ADD ALL THE REMAINING INGREDIENTS, except the sesame seeds, and mash the liquid into the spinach with a wooden spoon for 30 to 45 seconds. This bruising technique accomplishes a thorough mixing of the spinach and the dressing.

SPRINKLE THE SPINACH with the sesame seeds and serve immediately. Or chill the mixture until ready to serve and sprinkle with the sesame seeds just before serving. ◉

Grilled Romaine Lettuce

Fritz Sonnenschmidt

2 tablespoons grated fresh ginger

1 cup light soy sauce

4 tablespoons dry white wine

2 heaping tablespoons brown sugar

3 tablespoons toasted sesame oil

3 heads romaine lettuce, trimmed, washed, and cut in half lengthwise

PREHEAT A GAS GRILL to medium–high.

IN A BLENDER, combine the ginger, soy sauce, wine, brown sugar, and sesame oil, and process until well blended.

BRUSH THE ROMAINE halves with the marinade. Spray the romaine halves with nonstick cooking spray and place on the grill. Grill over medium heat for 2 to 3 minutes. Turn the romaine halves, brush with the marinade, and grill for 3 to 4 more minutes.

REMOVE THE ROMAINE from the grill and keep warm until ready to serve. ◉

Romaine lettuce is sturdy enough to be grilled alongside the other items for your barbecued meal, and is a delightful alternative to a salad. Fritz also likes to use this marinade for spareribs.

SERVES 6

Grilled Asparagus with Two Sauces

Chris Schlesinger | Reprinted from *License to Grill*, William Morrow and Company

Garlic Mayonnaise

2 large egg yolks

1 teaspoon minced garlic

2 tablespoons fresh lemon juice (about ½ lemon)

1 cup extra-virgin olive oil

1 tablespoon roughly chopped fresh basil

Salt and freshly ground black pepper to taste

Vinaigrette

½ cup extra-virgin olive oil

¼ cup fresh lemon juice (about ½ lemon)

1 tablespoon minced garlic

Salt and freshly ground black pepper to taste

25 to 30 spears asparagus, bottom ¼ inch trimmed

2 tablespoons olive oil

Salt and freshly ground black pepper to taste

TO MAKE THE MAYONNAISE: In a food processor, combine the egg yolks, garlic, and lemon juice and puree for about 10 seconds. With the motor running, add the oil in a steady stream; turn off the motor as soon as the oil is just incorporated. Add the basil and salt and pepper, pulse to combine, cover and refrigerate until ready to serve.

TO MAKE THE VINAIGRETTE: whisk all the ingredients together in a small bowl.

FILL YOUR SINK with water and ice. In a small stockpot, bring 6 quarts of water and a pinch of salt to a boil. Add half of the asparagus and cook for 3 minutes; it should remain bright green and firm. Immediately transfer the asparagus to the ice-water to stop the cooking process. Repeat the cooking and cooling process with the remaining asparagus.

DRAIN THE ASPARAGUS and toss it in a medium bowl with the olive oil and salt and pepper. Grill the asparagus over medium-high heat for 3 to 4 minutes, turning several times, until it is nicely browned. Serve with the mayonnaise or the vinaigrette. ◉

For Chris, the arrival of spring asparagus occurs at about the same time as the urge to liberate his grill from winter storage. To keep the asparagus's bright-green color, "blanch" or partially cook it, and plunge it into ice cold water before grilling. Two sauces are offered here: Mayonnaise is a classic choice, but if you are watching your cholesterol intake or are concerned about the raw eggs in your area, a light vinaigrette is also appealing.

SERVES 4

Grilled Red Cabbage

Fritz Sonnenschmidt

This dish tastes like its cousin, braised red cabbage, but it cooks up quicker and retains a crisper texture.

SERVES 8

1 medium head red cabbage

½ cup red wine vinegar

½ cup water

1 to 1½ tablespoons sugar

½ tablespoon salt

3 tablespoons vegetable oil

Salt and freshly ground black pepper to taste

WASH THE CABBAGE well and remove the tough outer leaves. Cut the cabbage into 8 wedges.

IN A LARGE BOWL, combine the vinegar, water, sugar, salt, and oil. Add the cabbage wedges and toss to coat well. Marinate the cabbage for 2 hours, turning it twice.

REMOVE THE CABBAGE WEDGES from the marinade and place on a grill over medium-high heat. Grill the cabbage for 10 to 15 minutes, until tender-crisp, turning occasionally. Season with salt and pepper. ◉

Garden Slaw

Marcel Desaulniers

Dressing

1½ tablespoons cider vinegar

1 tablespoon fresh lemon juice

1 teaspoon Dijon-style mustard

1 teaspoon hot pepper sauce

¼ teaspoon whole celery seeds

½ cup safflower oil

Salt and freshly ground black pepper to taste

½ small head green cabbage (about ¾ to 1 pound), discolored and tough outer leaves removed, washed, cored, quartered, and thinly sliced

½ small head red cabbage (about ¾ to 1 pound), discolored and tough outer leaves removed, washed, cored, quartered, and thinly sliced

¼ pound carrots, trimmed, peeled, and cut into 3-inch-long by ¼-inch-thick strips

1 medium red onion (about 6 ounces), peeled and thinly sliced

3 medium green bell peppers (about 6 ounces), washed, cut in half lengthwise, core removed, seeded, membrane removed, and cut into thin strips the length of the pepper

MAKE THE DRESSING: In a 7–quart stainless steel bowl, whisk together the cider vinegar, lemon juice, mustard, hot sauce, and whole celery seeds. Add the safflower oil in a slow, steady stream while whisking to incorporate. Adjust the seasonings with salt and pepper and whisk to combine.

ADD THE GREEN AND RED CABBAGES, carrots, red onion, and green peppers to the bowl. Toss to thoroughly combine. Cover the bowl tightly with plastic wrap and refrigerate until ready to serve (the slaw may be kept refrigerated in a covered noncorrosive container for up to 2 days before serving.) ◉

Here is Marcel's take on classic cole slaw. He favors a dressing that's vinaigrette-based rather than mayonnaise-based, and adds a lively dose of Dijon-style mustard, hot pepper sauce, and thinly sliced garden vegetables. A bonus: the slaw can be made up to two days before serving it.

SERVES 4

Sesame Stir-Fried Vegetables

Marcel Desaulniers

It's well worth your time
to seek fresh water chestnuts
from an Asian market.
Their skin is almost black
and must be peeled away
to reveal the creamy white
flesh underneath.

SERVES 4

½ pound snow peas, trimmed

1 tablespoon peanut oil

1 teaspoon toasted sesame oil

1 bunch scallions, cleaned, trimmed, and thinly sliced on the bias

½ medium head bok choy (about 1½ pounds), cored, sliced ¼-inch thick
   (white part only), and washed

½ pound fresh water chestnuts, peeled and sliced ⅛-inch thick

Salt and freshly ground black pepper to taste

3 tablespoons sesame seeds, toasted

HEAT 3 QUARTS of salted water in a 5-quart saucepan over medium–high heat
until boiling. Add the snow peas and cook for about 1 minute, until tender
but still very crisp. Drain the snow peas in a colander, then immediately
plunge into ice water to stop the cooking and keep the snow peas bright
green. Remove the peas from the ice water and drain thoroughly.

HEAT THE PEANUT OIL and the sesame oil in a large nonstick sauté pan (or in a
wok) over high heat. When the oil is hot, add the scallions and stir-fry for 30
seconds. Add the bok choy and water chestnuts, season with salt and pepper,
and stir-fry for 2½ minutes. Add the snow peas and stir-fry for 1½ minutes.
Add the toasted sesame seeds and toss to combine. ◉

Fresh Herb Couscous

Marcel Desaulniers

1 cup vegetable stock

1 tablespoon extra-virgin olive oil

½ teaspoon salt

¼ teaspoon freshly ground white pepper

1 cup instant couscous

1 tablespoon chopped fresh parsley

½ tablespoon chopped fresh thyme

½ teaspoon chopped fresh oregano

COMBINE THE VEGETABLE STOCK, olive oil, salt, and pepper in a 3-quart sauce-pan and bring to a boil over medium-high heat. Add the couscous to the boiling stock and stir to combine. Remove from the heat, cover with a lid or aluminum foil, and set aside for 5 minutes.

STIR THE CHOPPED HERBS into the couscous using a fork. ◉

Chopped fresh herbs add pizzaz to quick-cooking couscous for a side dish in an instant.

SERVES 4

Grits Cakes

Marcel Desaulniers

Classic Southern-style grits are jazzed-up with grated cheddar cheese and sweet white corn, then cooled and molded into individual patties. A short time in the oven yields cakes with a creamy interior and crispy, golden exterior.

SERVES 4

2 cups chicken stock

1 cup heavy cream

2 tablespoons unsalted butter

1 teaspoon salt

½ teaspoon freshly ground black pepper

1 cup stone-ground white grits

¼ cup grated cheddar cheese

½ cup fresh white corn kernels

HEAT THE CHICKEN STOCK, heavy cream, butter, salt, and pepper in a 3–quart saucepan over medium heat. Bring the mixture to a boil, then add the grits in a slow, steady stream while stirring constantly with a rigid wire whisk. Continue to stir while cooking the mixture for 6 minutes until very thick. Remove the grits mixture from the heat and add the cheese, stirring until the cheese melts and is incorporated. Add the corn and stir to combine.

POUR THE GRITS MIXTURE into a 10x15–inch nonstick baking sheet with sides, using a rubber spatula to spread the mixture to a uniform thickness. Place the baking sheet on a cooling rack and cool for 30 minutes at room temperature, then place the pan in the refrigerator for 1 hour, until the grits mixture is thoroughly chilled.

PREHEAT THE OVEN to 350°F.

REMOVE THE CHILLED MIXTURE from the refrigerator. Turn the baking sheet over onto a clean, dry cutting board, lifting the baking sheet off the inverted mixture. Cut the solidified grits mixture in half lengthwise across the center, then cut each half lengthwise in half. Now make 3 cuts widthwise through each section, giving you 12 portions. Use a metal spatula to place the cakes, evenly spaced, onto 2 clean, dry nonstick baking sheets.

PLACE THE BAKING SHEETS of grits cakes on the top oven rack and bake for 15 to 20 minutes, until the grits cakes are slightly crispy. ◉

Ricotta Soufflés

Fritz Sonnenschmidt

1½ cups milk

3½ ounces cornmeal

Salt and freshly ground black pepper to taste

3½ ounces ricotta cheese

4 tablespoons chopped fresh dill

8 ounces unsalted butter

4 eggs, separated

Fine dry bread crumbs for lining custard cups

IN A SAUCEPAN, bring the milk to a boil. Add the cornmeal, salt and pepper and cook, stirring, for 5 to 10 minutes, until thickened. Cool slightly.

STIR IN THE RICOTTA, dill, butter, and egg yolks and cool to room temperature.

IN A BOWL, whip the egg whites until stiff peaks form. Fold the egg whites into the cooled ricotta mixture.

BUTTER FOUR CUSTARD CUPS and dust with the bread crumbs. Divide the soufflé mixture among the custard cups.

PLACE THE CUSTARD CUPS in a baking pan and fill the pan with about ½ inch of water. Place the pan on a grill over low heat. Cover the grill and cook the soufflés for 20 to 30 minutes. ◉

Prepare the cornmeal-infused soufflé base in the kitchen and bring cups-full to the grill where they can bake in a water bath alongside the entrée.

SERVES 4

Curried Brown Rice

Marcel Desaulniers

Ordinary brown rice is revitalized Asian-style with curry powder, Japanese rice wine and sliced almonds. It is served cold as a salad, drizzled with a fragrant vinaigrette made with Szechwan peppercorns.

SERVES 4

3 tablespoons peanut oil

1 tablespoon curry powder

1 cup chopped scallions

1 cup brown rice

Salt and freshly ground black pepper to taste

2 cups hot vegetable stock

¼ cup sake (Japanese rice wine)

1 cup sliced almonds, toasted

½ cup Szechwan Peppercorn Vinaigrette, page 79

PREHEAT THE OVEN to 350°F.

HEAT 2 TABLESPOONS of the peanut oil in a 5-quart saucepan over medium-high heat. When the oil is hot, add the curry powder and cook, stirring constantly, for 1 minute. Add the scallions and cook for 1 minute. Add the brown rice, season with salt and pepper, and stir to coat the rice with the oil. Add the hot vegetable stock and stir to incorporate. Cover the saucepan and place in the preheated oven for 1 hour.

REMOVE THE PAN from the oven and immediately transfer the rice to a 5-quart stainless steel bowl.

IN A SMALL BOWL, whisk the sake with the remaining 1 tablespoon peanut oil. Add the sake–oil mixture to the rice and use a fork to stir and incorporate the mixture into the rice. Cool the rice to room temperature, stirring occasionally.

WHEN THE RICE has cooled to room temperature, add the sliced almonds, then stir to combine. Place the rice in the refrigerator to chill completely, about 1 hour.

PLACE THE RICE on serving plates and sprinkle each portion with 2 tablespoons of the vinaigrette. ◉

Orange-Sweet Potato Hobo Pack

Chris Schlesinger | Reprinted from *License to Grill*, William Morrow and Company

4 medium-sized sweet potatoes, washed but not peeled, cut into 2-inch-thick rounds

1 orange, thinly sliced (including peel)

1 large onion, peeled and quartered

⅓ cup raisins

¼ cup olive oil

¼ cup unsalted butter, cut into small bits

Salt and freshly ground black pepper to taste

⅓ cup fresh lemon juice (about 1 large lemon)

⅓ cup honey

⅓ cup roughly chopped fresh parsley

IN A LARGE BOWL, combine the sweet potatoes, orange, onion, raisins, olive oil, and butter. Toss lightly, sprinkle with salt and pepper to taste, and toss again.

LAY OUT TWO SHEETS of heavy-duty foil, each about two-feet long, one on top of the other. Place the sweet potato mixture in the center, then lay a third length of heavy-duty foil over the top. Fold the edges of the sheets together on all sides, closing the pack, then roll them up until they bump into the food, forming a ridge around its perimeter. Place the pack right-side up in the center of a fourth length of foil and fold the four sides over the top of the packet, one after another.

NOW THE PACKAGE is ready for the coals. The fire should have passed its peak of intensity and be dying down, so that it consists primarily of glowing coals covered with a thin film of gray ash, but very few flickering flames—in other words, you want a medium to low dying fire. Clear a place for the foil packet, leaving a thin layer of coals. Place the packet on the cleared area and heap up the coals all around, but not directly on top. Cook, keeping watch and shifting the packet as needed so it is continuously in contact with glowing coals, for 30 to 35 minutes, depending on the intensity of the coals.

MIX THE LEMON JUICE, honey, and parsley in a small bowl.

REMOVE THE FOIL PACK from the coals, unroll the foil, drizzle the vegetables with the lemon-honey mixture, and serve at once. ◑

Don't be alarmed by the appearance of the blackened foil package when you pull it out of the fire. It will only add drama to the moment when you set the pack in front of your guests and open it, releasing the heady aromas of the slow-roasted vegetables and fruits.

SERVES 4

Grilled Sweet Potato Coins

Fritz Sonnenschmidt | Recipe Courtesy of the Weber-Stephen Products Co.

2 small sweet potatoes (about 1 pound total)

¼ cup vegetable oil

1 teaspoon salt

IN A 2-QUART SAUCEPAN, bring 1 quart of salted water to a boil.

PEEL THE SWEET POTATOES and slice into ¼- to ½-inch-thick disks. Add the sweet potato disks to the boiling water and cook for 2 to 3 minutes.

REMOVE THE PARTIALLY cooked sweet potatoes from the water and plunge into a bowl of ice water.

REMOVE THE SWEET POTATOES from the water, pat dry, and place in a bowl or large plastic bag. Pour the oil over the sweet potatoes and toss to coat.

GRILL THE SWEET POTATOES over medium-high heat for 4 to 6 minutes on each side. Remove the sweet potatoes from the grill and sprinkle with salt. ◉

Simply prepared, but addicting, these are a terrific change of pace from regular potatoes. Partially cooking the sweet potatoes in water before grilling is an important step. You can do it ahead of time, if you wish.

SERVES 4

Grilled Caraway Potatoes

Fritz Sonnenschmidt

8 medium russet potatoes

2 tablespoons vegetable oil

½ teaspoon salt

1 to 2 teaspoons caraway seeds

IN A LARGE SAUCEPAN, boil the potatoes in water until just slightly underdone. Drain the potatoes and let stand until cool enough to handle.

PEEL THE POTATOES and cut in half lengthwise.

PLACE THE POTATOES in a bowl. Add the oil, salt and caraway seeds and toss to coat well.

PLACE THE POTATOES on a grill over medium–high heat. Grill for about 4 minutes on each side. ◉

Caraway seeds add a Germanic flair to uncom-plicated grilled potatoes. A brief time in boiling water before grilling is necessary to ensure even cooking of the potatoes.

SERVES 8

Grilled Potatoes with Yogurt–Parsley Sauce

Chris Schlesinger | Reprinted from *License to Grill*, William Morrow and Company

Serve these potatoes as a complement to Middle Eastern-flavored entrées. After partially cooking them in boiling water, grill the potatoes long enough to get a good brown crust on the outside, which will add texture and smoky flavor to the dish.

SERVES 4

4 medium potatoes of your choice, cut into rounds about 1-inch thick

¼ cup olive oil

Salt and freshly ground black pepper to taste

1 cup plain yogurt

¼ cup fresh lemon juice (about 1 lemon)

2 tablespoons cumin seeds, toasted if you want, or 1 tablespoon ground cumin

1 cup fresh parsley leaves

4 cloves garlic

⅓ cup extra-virgin olive oil

IN A MEDIUM SAUCEPAN, bring 1 quart of salted water to a boil over high heat. Add the sliced potatoes and boil for 8 to 10 minutes until you can easily stick a fork through them, but still feel some resistance; the slices should not break apart easily. Drain and cool to room temperature.

TOSS THE COOLED POTATO slices in a medium bowl with the olive oil and salt and pepper to taste, then place the potatoes on the grill over medium heat. Cook for about 3 minutes on each side, or until nicely browned.

REMOVE THE POTATOES from the grill and put them in a medium bowl. Add the yogurt, lemon juice, and cumin, toss well, and set aside.

PLACE THE PARSLEY and garlic in a food processor and puree until smooth. With the motor running, slowly drizzle in the olive oil until just incorporated. Just before serving, drizzle the garlic–parsley mixture over the potatoes. ◉

Grilled Spicy New Potato Salad

Chris Schlesinger | Reprinted from *License to Grill*, William Morrow and Company

16 new potatoes, about the size of golf balls

¼ cup olive oil

Salt and freshly ground black pepper to taste

⅓ cup extra-virgin olive oil

¼ cup mustard seeds, toasted if you want

¼ cup roughly chopped fresh parsley

1 tablespoon minced garlic

2 tablespoons fresh lemon juice (about ½ lemon)

6 to 16 dashes Tabasco sauce, depending on your taste

IN A LARGE SAUCEPAN, bring 2 quarts of salted water to a rapid boil over high heat. Add the potatoes and cook for about 15 minutes, or until the potatoes can be pierced with a fork but still offer considerable resistance—you want them to be firm but not crunchy. Drain the potatoes, run under cold water, and drain again.

HALVE THE POTATOES and thread them onto skewers, with the cut sides all facing the same way. Rub the potatoes lightly with the ¼ cup olive oil, sprinkle with salt and pepper, and place them on the grill over medium–high heat. Cook for 3 to 5 minutes, or until golden brown.

SLIDE THE POTATOES off the skewers into a medium bowl and add the remaining ingredients. Season to taste and toss well. This dish can be served warm or cold; it will keep, covered and refrigerated, for 3 to 4 days. ◉

Potatoes the size of golf balls are pierced and fired over hot coals. This treatment gives them crispy golden exteriors, which are offset brilliantly by the piquant ingredients with which they are tossed.

SERVES 4

Red Potato Salad

Marcel Desaulniers

Look for red-skinned potatoes in the supermarket and choose ones that are uniform in size, to ensure even cooking, and relatively blemish-free. Look for Pommery mustard at a specialty food store.

SERVES 4

1 tablespoon red wine vinegar

1 tablespoon Moutarde de Meaux Pommery mustard

¼ cup plus 1 teaspoon extra-virgin olive oil

2 tablespoons safflower oil

Salt and freshly ground black pepper to taste

3 pounds red-skinned potatoes, washed, but not peeled

1 medium red onion (about 6 ounces), peeled and thinly sliced

2 tablespoons chopped fresh parsley

PREPARE THE DRESSING: whisk together, in a 3-quart stainless steel bowl, the red wine vinegar and Meaux mustard until combined. Add ¼ cup olive oil in a slow, steady stream, while whisking until incorporated, followed by the safflower oil, still whisking until combined. Add the salt and pepper and whisk to combine. Cover tightly with plastic wrap and set aside at room temperature until needed.

PLACE THE POTATOES in a 6-quart saucepan and cover with cold water. Bring to a simmer over medium-high heat, then adjust the heat to simmer slowly until the potatoes are cooked through, about 20 to 22 minutes. Drain the hot water from the potatoes, then cool the potatoes in the saucepan under cold running water.

THOROUGHLY DRAIN the potatoes in a colander. Cut the potatoes into 1-inch cubes and transfer to a 7-quart stainless steel bowl. Season with salt and pepper. Add the sliced onion and parsley and toss to combine.

VIGOROUSLY WHISK the vinaigrette, add to the potatoes, and use a rubber spatula to combine the ingredients until the potatoes and onions are coated with the vinaigrette. Set aside at room temperature, loosely covered with plastic wrap, for up to 2 hours before serving. ◉

Black-Eyed Pea Salad

Marcel Desaulniers

¼ cup dried black-eyed peas, washed and picked over

1 cup extra-virgin olive oil

¼ cup cider vinegar

2 tablespoons Dijon-style mustard

1 teaspoon salt

1 teaspoon freshly ground black pepper

1 green bell pepper, washed, cut in half lengthwise, core removed, seeded, membrane removed, and cut into ¼-inch pieces

1 medium red onion, peeled and thinly sliced

SOAK THE BLACK-EYED PEAS overnight in 1 quart cold water.

DRAIN AND RINSE the soaked peas. Place the peas in a 2-quart saucepan and cover with 1 quart lightly salted water. Bring to a boil over high heat. Adjust the heat and simmer the peas until tender, about 30 to 35 minutes. Drain the peas, transfer to a dinner plate, and place uncovered in the refrigerator to cool.

IN A 5-QUART stainless steel bowl, whisk together the olive oil, cider vinegar, mustard, salt, and pepper. Add the cooled black-eyed peas, green pepper pieces, and sliced red onion. Use a rubber spatula to combine thoroughly. Cover the bowl with plastic wrap and refrigerate until needed. ◉

Black-eyed peas make a savory Southern-style salad when tossed with a tangy vinaigrette. Diced green peppers and red onions add lively color to the mix.

SERVES 4

Grilled Shrimp and Black Bean Salad with Papaya-Chile Dressing

Chris Schlesinger | Reprinted from *License to Grill*, William Morrow and Company

1 ripe papaya, peeled and seeds removed

½ cup fresh lime juice (about 4 limes)

½ cup olive oil

1 tablespoon minced garlic

2 tablespoons minced fresh chile pepper of your choice

2 tablespoons cumin seeds, toasted if you want, or 1 tablespoon ground cumin

Salt and freshly ground black pepper to taste

1 cup dried black beans, soaked in water to cover overnight, or at least 5 hours, or one 15-ounce can black beans

16 medium shrimp (about 1 pound), peeled, deveined, and tails removed

1 tablespoon vegetable oil

2 avocados, peeled, pitted, and diced medium

2 tomatoes about the size of baseballs, cored and diced medium

1 red onion, peeled and diced small

½ cup roughly chopped fresh cilantro

MAKE THE DRESSING: In food processor or blender, combine the papaya, lime juice, oil, garlic, chile, cumin, salt, and pepper, and puree until smooth. Cover and refrigerate.

IF USING DRIED BEANS, drain them, rinse them well, and place them in a medium saucepan with enough water to cover by about 1 inch. Bring to a boil over high heat, reduce the heat to medium, and simmer, adding small amounts of water as needed, for 3 hours, or until just soft to the bite but not mushy, drain and cool. If using canned beans, drain and rinse them well.

continued on next page

This salad, full of Latin flavors, tastes best when eaten just after being made. Chris recommends preparing all of the ingredients ahead of time and putting them together at the last minute.

SERVES 4

Grilled Shrimp and Black Bean Salad
with Papaya-Chile Dressing (continued)

BRUSH THE SHRIMP lightly with the vegetable oil, sprinkle with salt and pepper to taste, and thread onto skewers. Grill the shrimp over a medium-hot fire for 3 to 4 minutes per side. To check for doneness: Cut into one of the shrimp and check to see that it is opaque all the way through. Remove from the grill and, as soon as the shrimp are cool enough to handle, remove them from the skewers and cut each one into 3 pieces.

IN A MEDIUM BOWL, combine the shrimp, black beans, avocados, tomatoes, onion, and cilantro. Stir the dressing well, pour in just enough to lightly coat all the ingredients, toss well, and serve. This salad will keep, covered and refrigerated, for 3 days. ◉

Grilled Bread Salad with Grilled Figs

Chris Schlesinger | Reprinted from *License to Grill*, William Morrow and Company

1 tablespoon fresh lemon juice

¼ cup olive oil

¼ cup balsamic vinegar

1 tablespoon minced garlic

Salt and freshly ground black pepper to taste

1 baguette or other long crusty loaf of bread

6 fresh figs, halved

1 tablespoon olive oil

1 red onion, peeled and diced large

10 basil leaves, cut into long thin strips

2 tablespoons roughly chopped fresh parsley

2 roasted red peppers, diced large

MAKE THE DRESSING: In a small bowl, combine the lemon juice, olive oil, balsamic vinegar, garlic, salt, and pepper, whisk together well, and set aside.

CUT THE LOAF of bread in half lengthwise, and place on the grill around the edge of a medium–hot fire, where the heat is low, and cook until browned, 5 minutes per side. Don't be impatient–toast the bread slowly on both sides so it dries out and becomes very crusty. When the bread is well toasted, remove it from the grill and cut into medium–sized chunks. You should have 5 cups.

MEANWHILE, PLACE THE FIGS in a small bowl with 1 tablespoon oil and salt and pepper to taste and toss well. Place the figs on the grill, cut–side down, over the medium–hot fire and cook, turning once or twice, until browned, 2 to 3 minutes.

IN A LARGE BOWL, combine the toasted bread and grilled figs with the onion, basil, parsley, and roasted red peppers. Stir the dressing well, pour just enough into the bowl to moisten the ingredients, and toss well. Season to taste with salt and pepper, allow to sit about 10 minutes so the bread absorbs some of the dressing, toss again, and serve. ◉

When grilled, figs take on a smoky, caramelized character. It's important to toast the bread completely on the grill so that it will absorb the dressing without instantly becoming soggy.

SERVES 4 TO 6

Grilled Chicken and Mango Salad

Chris Schlesinger | Reprinted from *License to Grill*, William Morrow and Company

This Thai-style salad features an abundance of flavors and textures. Look for fish sauce, labeled as *nam pla*, in the international section of the supermarket or in an Asian market.

SERVES 4

½ cup unsalted peanuts

2 whole boneless, skinless chicken breasts (each 10 to 12 ounces)

2 tablespoons vegetable oil

Salt and freshly ground black pepper to taste

2 ripe mangos, peeled, pitted, and diced medium

1 cup seedless green or red grapes, halved

1 small red onion, peeled and diced large

½ red bell pepper, seeded and diced large

¼ cup roughly chopped fresh cilantro (or substitute parsley)

2 tablespoons roughly chopped fresh basil

6 tablespoons fresh orange juice (about 1 small orange)

¼ cup fresh lime juice (about 2 limes)

1 tablespoon fish sauce (optional)

2 tablespoons minced fresh chile pepper of your choice

1 tablespoon minced fresh ginger

TOAST THE PEANUTS on a baking sheet in a 350°F oven until golden brown, about 10 minutes, then roughly chop. Set aside.

RUB THE CHICKEN BREASTS lightly with oil, sprinkle with salt and pepper to taste, and place on the grill over medium-high heat. Cook for 7 to 9 minutes on each side. To check for doneness: Cut into the thickest part and peek inside to be sure they are opaque all the way through, with no pink.

AS SOON AS THEY are cool enough to handle, cut the grilled chicken breasts into bite-sized chunks and place in a large bowl. Add the mangos, grapes, red onion, bell pepper, cilantro, and basil and set aside.

MAKE THE DRESSING: In a small bowl, combine the orange juice, lime juice, fish sauce, if using, chile, ginger, salt, and pepper, and whisk together well.

ADD JUST ENOUGH DRESSING to the chicken-mango mixture to moisten the ingredients, toss well, and season to taste with salt and pepper. Sprinkle with the chopped peanuts and serve. ◉

Poultry

Grilled Chicken and Eggplant with North African Flavors

Chris Schlesinger | Reprinted from *License to Grill*, William Morrow and Company

4 whole boneless chicken breasts (each 8 to 12 ounces)

Salt and freshly ground black pepper to taste

1 red bell pepper, halved and seeded

1 green bell pepper, halved and seeded

1 red onion, peeled and cut into rings about ½-inch thick

1 medium eggplant, cut lengthwise into planks about ½-inch thick

¼ cup vegetable oil

⅓ cup fresh lemon juice (about 1½ lemons)

⅓ cup olive oil

1 large tomato, cored and diced large

½ cup good-quality green or black olives, pitted

2 tablespoons minced garlic

2 tablespoons minced fresh chile pepper of your choice

½ cup roughly chopped fresh parsley

¼ cup cumin seeds, toasted if you want, or 2 tablespoons ground cumin

SPRINKLE THE CHICKEN BREASTS with salt and pepper to taste and grill over medium–high heat, skin–side down, for 8 to 10 minutes. Flip and grill for an additional 5 to 6 minutes. To check for doneness: Cut into one of the breasts at the thickest point and check to see that it is opaque all the way through with no redness.

MEANWHILE, IN A SMALL BOWL, combine the bell peppers, onion, eggplant, vegetable oil, and salt and pepper to taste and toss to coat the vegetables. Place the vegetables on the grill and cook until browned and softened, 3 to 4 minutes per side.

WHEN THE CHICKEN and vegetables are done, remove them from the grill and, as soon as they are cool enough to handle, cut them into large chunks. Place the chicken and vegetables in a large bowl, add all the remaining ingredients, and toss well. Season to taste with salt and pepper and serve. ◉

Chicken and vegetables are grilled, then tossed with flavorful ingredients, and served immediately. Every bite will contain a melange of Moroccan-style flavors. Chris calls this method "the bowl technique."

SERVES 4

Peach and Chicken Skewers with Middle Eastern Shake and Simple Raisin Sauce

Chris Schlesinger | Reprinted from *License to Grill*, William Morrow and Company

Chris's "shake" is a combination of freshly ground potent spices that are sprinkled onto the chicken and peach chunks just before eating. Pour the extras into a salt shaker so that your guests can add more spices as they like. Take care not to thread the chicken and peaches onto the skewers too tightly or it might prevent the chicken from cooking properly.

SERVES 2 AS ENTRéE, 4 AS APPETIZER

Simple Raisin Sauce

⅓ *cup olive oil*

¼ *cup raisins, roughly chopped*

¼ *cup fresh lime juice (about 2 limes)*

Salt and freshly ground black pepper to taste

Middle Eastern Shake

2 tablespoons cumin seeds, toasted if you want, or 1 tablespoon ground cumin

2 tablespoons coriander seeds, toasted along with the cumin seeds if you want,
   or 1 tablespoon ground coriander

Pinch of ground cinnamon

1 tablespoon kosher salt

1 tablespoon freshly cracked black pepper

3 tablespoons vegetable oil

1 tablespoon minced garlic

¼ *cup roughly chopped fresh cilantro*

Salt and freshly ground black pepper to taste

1 pound boneless, skinless chicken breasts, cut into large chunks (about 16 chunks)

2 peaches, pitted and cut into eighths

2 red bell peppers, halved, seeded, and halves quartered

MAKE THE SAUCE: In a small bowl, combine all the ingredients. Whisk together well and set aside.

MAKE THE SHAKE: In a small bowl, combine all the ingredients, mix well, and set aside.

IN A MEDIUM BOWL, combine the vegetable oil, garlic, cilantro, and salt and pepper to taste. Add the chicken chunks and toss until well coated. Thread the chicken onto 4 skewers alternately with the peaches and pepper pieces. Place the skewers on the grill over medium–high heat, and cook for 5 to 7 minutes per side. To check for doneness: Cut into one of the pieces of chicken and check to be sure it is opaque all the way through.

REMOVE THE SKEWERS from the grill and place them on a platter. Pour the sauce over the top, sprinkle with the shake, and serve hot. ◉

Grilled Spicy Chicken Legs with Garden Slaw

Marcel Desaulniers

Cayenne pepper lends its mighty flavor to a dry seasoning mixture that coats chicken legs. Before grilling, the chicken legs are oven-braised in dark beer to infuse them with another dimension of flavor. Then, they can either be barbecued immediately or refrigerated until the party starts.

SERVES 4

1 tablespoon dry mustard

1 tablespoon salt

1 teaspoon ground celery seeds

½ teaspoon ground cayenne pepper

½ teaspoon ground white pepper

4 chicken leg and thigh portions

1 cup dark beer

1 cup barbecue sauce

Garden Slaw, page 39

PREHEAT THE OVEN to 300°F.

IN A SMALL BOWL, combine the mustard, salt, ground celery seeds, cayenne pepper, and white pepper.

PLACE THE CHICKEN in a baking dish. Sprinkle the dry seasoning mixture over the chicken, coating all sides. Pour the beer into the baking dish and cover with a lid or aluminum foil. Place the baking dish in the preheated oven and cook the chicken for 45 minutes. Remove the dish from the oven. Transfer the chicken to a clean dish. The chicken can be grilled immediately, or cooled to room temperature, covered with plastic wrap, and refrigerated for up to 24 hours before grilling.

GRILL THE CHICKEN LEGS over medium–low heat for 5 to 7 minutes, turning as necessary to prevent overcharring. Baste the legs with the barbecue sauce, while continuing to cook and turn the legs for 5 to 7 more minutes. Remove the legs from the grill. Serve immediately (or keep warm in a preheated 200°F oven for up to 30 minutes), accompanied by the Garden Slaw. ◉

Grilled Chicken Legs in Buttermilk

Fritz Sonnenschmidt

Though this dish is simple to prepare, be sure to plan ahead. The chicken must marinate in its buttermilk pool for two days in order to obtain the proper flavor. Don't discard the marinade when removing the chicken. After adding a few ingredients and reducing slightly, the marinade doubles as a creamy, raisin-flecked sauce.

SERVES 4

4 chicken legs

Salt and freshly ground black pepper to taste

Juice from ½ lemon

1 pint buttermilk

2 tablespoons vegetable oil

4 ounces raisins

4 tablespoons dry white wine

1 cup dry red wine

Grilled Caraway Potatoes, page 47

Grilled Red Cabbage, page 38

PLACE THE CHICKEN LEGS in a shallow dish. Season the chicken with salt and pepper and sprinkle with the lemon juice. Add the buttermilk to the dish, cover, and refrigerate for 2 days, turning occasionally.

REMOVE THE CHICKEN from the marinade and pat dry with paper towels. Reserve the marinade.

BRUSH THE CHICKEN with oil and place on a grill over medium–high heat. Grill the chicken for 20 to 25 minutes, or until the juices run clear when pierced with the tip of a knife.

WHILE THE CHICKEN is cooking, soak the raisins in white wine.

IN A SAUCEPAN, heat the reserved marinade and red wine over high heat until reduced by one-third. Drain the raisins, add the raisins to the pan and bring the mixture to a boil. Adjust the seasonings.

SERVE THE CHICKEN with the raisin sauce, accompanied by the Grilled Caraway Potatoes and Grilled Red Cabbage. ◉

Mustard-Grilled Chicken with Tomatoes, Corn, and Grits Cakes

Marcel Desaulniers

½ cup whole-grain mustard

4 tablespoons dry white wine

2 tablespoons sour cream

4 chicken breast halves with skin

Salt and freshly ground black pepper to taste

1½ cups fresh white corn kernels

4 medium tomatoes, peeled, seeded, and chopped into ¼-inch pieces

Grits Cakes, page 42

AT LEAST 1 DAY before serving, prepare the marinade by whisking together in a 3-quart stainless steel bowl the mustard, white wine, and sour cream. Season the chicken breasts with salt and pepper. Place the chicken breasts in a 5-quart plastic container. Pour the marinade over the chicken and turn to coat thoroughly. Seal the container and refrigerate until ready to grill, at least 24 hours.

PREHEAT THE OVEN to 350°F.

GRILL THE CHICKEN over medium heat for 15 minutes. Turn the chicken as necessary to prevent overcharring. Transfer the breasts to a baking sheet and place on the center rack of the preheated oven.

WHILE THE CHICKEN is cooking, heat the corn and tomato pieces in a large nonstick sauté pan over medium-high heat. Season with salt and pepper and sauté until hot.

PLACE 3 CRISPY GRITS CAKES on each of 4 serving plates. Place an equal amount of the tomato and corn mixture over the grits cakes. Place a chicken breast in the center of each plate and serve immediately. ◉

Marinating in a creamy mustard-based mixture for 24 hours lends moisture and flavor to plain-old chicken breasts. Late summer is the best time to make this dish, when tomatoes and corn are at the height of their season.

SERVES 4

Grilled Mandarin Duck Breasts with Sesame Stir-Fried Vegetables

Marcel Desaulniers

Four 3- to 4-ounce boneless, skinless duck breasts, trimmed of
*   excess fat and membrane*

¼ cup fresh orange juice

2 tablespoons rice vinegar

2 teaspoons soy sauce

Salt and freshly ground black pepper to taste

Sesame Stir-Fried Vegetables, page 40

PREHEAT THE OVEN to 225° F.

PLACE THE DUCK BREASTS, one at a time, between two sheets of lightly oiled aluminum foil or parchment paper. Slightly flatten each breast using a meat cleaver or the bottom of a heavy-duty sauté pan.

IN A 3-QUART stainless steel bowl, whisk together the orange juice, rice vinegar, and soy sauce. Place the duck breasts in the marinade, then season the breasts with salt and pepper.

GRILL THE DUCK BREASTS over medium heat for 2 to 2½ minutes on each side. Transfer the grilled duck breasts to a baking sheet and hold in the preheated oven until ready to serve.

DIVIDE THE SESAME Stir-Fried Vegetables among 4 serving plates.

SLICE THE DUCK BREASTS at a slight angle across the grain. Arrange each sliced duck breast in a fan in the center of the vegetables and serve immediately. ◉

Mild Chinese flavors flatter quickly grilled duck. Flattening the duck breasts helps them cook rapidly and evenly.

SERVES 4

Grilled Duck, Peking-Style

Fritz Sonnenschmidt

One 4- to 5-pound duck, thawed if frozen, all fat removed

2 tablespoons brown sugar

4 shallots, roughly chopped

2 cloves garlic, roughly chopped

1 inch fresh ginger, roughly chopped

Asian pancakes

Dipping sauce of your choice

Grilled Romaine Lettuce, page 35

REMOVE THE NECK and giblets from the duck cavity. Rinse the duck carefully with cold water inside and out and pat dry with paper towels.

IN A SMALL BOWL, mix the brown sugar with a small amount of water. Brush the sugar mixture over the entire duck.

MAKE A SMALL INCISION in the duck skin near the neck. Place a drinking straw into the incision and blow like you are blowing up a balloon. The duck skin will separate from the duck meat.

PLACE THE SHALLOTS, garlic, and ginger into the duck cavity. Close the cavity with a wooden skewer. Truss the duck and place on a roasting rack in a roasting pan. Refrigerate uncovered for 24 hours.

HEAT A GAS GRILL to medium–hot. Spray the duck with nonstick cooking spray and place on the grill. Grill the duck for 2½ hours, turning occasionally. For the last 10 minutes of cooking time, increase the heat to high.

REMOVE THE DUCK from grill and let stand for 5 minutes. Slice the duck meat and arrange on a platter. Serve with Asian pancakes, dipping sauce, and Grilled Romaine Lettuce. ◉

Read on to discover Fritz's secret for making crisp Peking-style duck: An ordinary drinking straw is used to separate the duck skin from the meat, which allows air to circulate on both sides of the skin. Then, the duck is dried for 24 hours in the refrigerator. Look for the thin pancakes that traditionally accompany Peking duck in an Asian market.

SERVES 6

Tea-Smoked Duck

Fritz Sonnenschmidt | Recipe Courtesy of the Weber-Stephen Products Co.

One 4- to 5-pound duck, thawed if frozen, all fat removed

¼ cup dry sherry

1½ teaspoons kosher salt

1 tablespoon finely chopped fresh ginger

2 scallions, coarsely chopped

2 whole star anise, crushed

1 to 2 teaspoons coarsely ground black pepper

⅓ cup black tea leaves

5 tablespoons uncooked white rice

3 tablespoons packed brown sugar

1 scallion, slivered (optional)

⅓ teaspoon ground coriander (optional)

Spicy Garlic in Eggplant Sauce, page 28

Cooked Chinese rice or egg noodles

REMOVE THE NECK and giblets from the duck cavity; rinse and pat dry. Pierce the duck all over with a fork. Truss the duck tightly.

IN A SMALL BOWL, combine the sherry, salt, ginger, chopped scallions, star anise, and pepper.

PLACE THE DUCK in a large plastic resealable bag. Add the sherry mixture and rub it inside the duck cavity and on the skin. Close the bag and marinate the duck in the refrigerator for 6 to 8 hours, or overnight.

MIX THE TEA, rice, and brown sugar in either a small foil pan or a heavy-duty aluminum foil packet. Close the foil packet loosely so the smoke can escape; leave the foil pan uncovered.

REMOVE THE MARINATED DUCK from the bag and pat dry.

continued on next page

Cooking smoked meats, poultry, or fish on an outdoor grill won't fill your kitchen with smoke odors and is easy to clean up. Perhaps new to you, smoking items with tea is an age-old Chinese tradition.

SERVES 6

Tea-Smoked Duck (continued)

FOR CHARCOAL GRILLS, place the foil pan or packet directly on the prepared coals over medium heat. Insert the cooking grate.

FOR GAS GRILLS, remove one cooking grate and center the remaining cooking grate on the grill. Place the foil pan or packet in the front left corner of the grill directly over the heat source.

PLACE THE DUCK, breast-side up, in the center of the grill's cooking grate over medium-high heat. Grill the duck for 1½ to 2 hours, or until a meat thermometer inserted into the thigh registers 180°F and the juices run clear. The smoke may not last the entire cooking time, but it will be sufficient to flavor the bird.

REMOVE THE COOKED DUCK from the grill and let stand for 10 minutes. Carve the duck into serving portions and sprinkle with the slivered scallions and coriander, if desired. Serve with Spicy Eggplant in Garlic Sauce and cooked Chinese rice or egg noodles. ◉

Honey-Charred Duck Breasts with Red Potato Salad

Marcel Desaulniers

Four 3- to 4-ounce boneless, skinless duck breasts, trimmed of
excess fat and membrane

¼ cup extra-virgin olive oil

2 tablespoons balsamic vinegar

2 tablespoons honey

1 tablespoon freshly cracked black peppercorns

Salt and freshly ground black pepper to taste

Red Potato Salad, page 50

PREHEAT THE OVEN to 350°F.

PLACE THE DUCK BREASTS, one at a time, between two sheets of lightly oiled aluminum foil or parchment paper. Slightly flatten each breast using a meat cleaver or the bottom of a heavy-duty sauté pan.

IN A 3-QUART stainless steel bowl, whisk together the olive oil, balsamic vinegar, honey, and cracked black peppercorns. Whisk to combine. Place the duck breasts in the marinade and stir to coat.

REMOVE THE DUCK BREASTS from the marinade then season the breasts with salt and freshly ground black pepper.

GRILL THE DUCK BREASTS over high heat for 2 minutes on each side. Remove the breasts from the grill and transfer to a nonstick baking sheet. Place the baking sheet in the preheated oven and cook the breasts for 10 minutes (this will yield medium-rare to medium duck; cook longer for duck that is more well-done).

TRANSFER THE BREASTS to a cutting board and use a sharp slicer to slice each breast into thin slices at a slight angle across the grain. Serve the warm sliced duck with the potato salad. ◉

Sweet and smoky flavors are good foils to rich, meaty duck breasts. This recipe shows how the simplest ingredients can often make the best dishes.

SERVES 4

Grilled Quail with Peppered Honey Peaches

Marcel Desaulniers

Peaches bathed in a whiskey, honey and peppercorn solution are a distinctive accompaniment to simple grilled quail.

SERVES 4

8 small peaches (about 3 ounces each)

3 tablespoons sour mash whiskey

3 tablespoons honey

2 teaspoons freshly cracked black pepper

8 whole quail, partially boned

2 tablespoons peanut oil

Salt and freshly ground black pepper to taste

1 medium bunch watercress, trimmed, washed, and dried

WASH THE PEACHES, cut in half and remove the pits. Cut each pitted peach half lengthwise into 6 slices. Set aside.

HEAT THE WHISKEY to a boil in a medium nonstick sauté pan over medium heat, add the honey and stir to combine. Heat the mixture for exactly 2 minutes, then immediately remove from the heat. Add the peach slices. Sprinkle the cracked black pepper over the peaches. Use a rubber spatula to gently coat the peaches with the honey–whiskey mixture. Transfer the peaches to a 3-quart stainless steel bowl, cover with plastic wrap, and set aside at room temperature for up to 2 to 3 hours before serving. (Once cooled to room temperature, the peaches may be refrigerated for up to 12 hours before serving.)

LIGHTLY COAT EACH QUAIL with peanut oil. Generously season the quail with salt and pepper.

GRILL THE QUAIL, breast-side down, over medium heat for 5 to 6 minutes until nicely browned, then turn the quail and grill for another 5 to 6 minutes.

SERVE THE GRILLED QUAIL accompanied by the peppered honey peaches. Garnish with the watercress. ◉

Seafood

Basic Grilled Whole Fish

Chris Schlesinger | Reprinted from *License to Grill*, William Morrow and Company

Four 1½ pound whole fish, cleaned and scaled

¼ cup vegetable oil

Salt and freshly ground black pepper to taste

2 lemons, quartered

MAKE SEVERAL DIAGONAL SLASHES about 1-inch deep along the sides of each fish. Rub the fish lightly with the oil and sprinkle generously inside and out with salt and pepper.

MAKE SURE THAT your grill grid is very clean, and place it on the fire at least 10 minutes before you are ready to cook; the easiest thing is just to put the grid over the coals right after you light them.

PLACE THE FISH directly on the grill over medium-high heat and grill for 4 to 5 minutes without moving them. It's very important not to mess with the fish at this time, because if a sear has not developed on the skin, the fish will stick. (If the fire is too hot and the fish seem to be burning, though, you may have to move them to a spot with less heat.) After 4 or 5 minutes, use tongs to gently free the fish from the grill grid, but don't turn them yet–continue to cook for another 2 to 3 minutes.

ROLL THE FISH over gently, and let cook for another 10 minutes or so. To check for doneness: Cut into one of the fish at the thickest part and check to see that it is opaque throughout.

REMOVE THE FISH from the grill, squeeze a lemon quarter or two over the top of each, and serve at once. ◉

Don't be discouraged if during your first couple of tries, your grilled fish end up less than whole. The smoky fish bits will still taste good. Follow Chris's instructions exactly and keep practicing—you'll soon get it right. Once perfected, you can try different rubs and stuffings. Choose red snapper, trout, ocean perch, bluefish, tilapia, mackerel, hybrid striped bass, tautog, or scud.

SERVES 4

Grilled Curry-Scented Shrimp and Red Onions with Curried Brown Rice

Marcel Desaulniers

1 large red onion (about ¾ pound), peeled and cut into ½-inch-thick slices

3 tablespoons extra-virgin olive oil

Salt and freshly ground black pepper to taste

Szechwan Peppercorn Vinaigrette, follows

1 pound large shrimp, peeled, deveined, and split in half lengthwise

½ teaspoon curry powder

Curried Brown Rice, page 44

BRUSH THE ONION slices with 2 tablespoons of the extra-virgin olive oil and season generously with salt and pepper. Grill the onion slices over medium heat until nicely charred and cooked through, about 3½ to 4 minutes on each side. Transfer the onions to a warm platter and drizzle with 3 tablespoons of the vinaigrette.

DIVIDE THE SHRIMP into four 4-ounce portions. Thread the shrimp onto 4 skewers. Brush the shrimp with the remaining tablespoon of olive oil. Season with salt and pepper, then evenly sprinkle the curry powder over the shrimp. Grill the shrimp skewers over medium heat for 1½ to 2 minutes on each side (a total of 3 to 4 minutes); be careful not to overcook. Place an equal amount of Curried Brown Rice onto 4 dinner plates. Whisk the vinaigrette. Sprinkle each portion of rice with 2 tablespoons of the vinaigrette.

ARRANGE THE GRILLED ONIONS around each portion of rice. Remove the shrimp from the skewers and place on the rice. Serve immediately. ◉

Shrimp cooks quickly, so pay close attention while it is grilling. As Marcel says, "shrimp can go from tender to tough in a matter of seconds." Szechwan peppercorns are not actually peppercorns at all, but rather small black berries of an ash tree common to the Szechwan province of China. Toasting them brings out their exotic flavor and aroma.

SERVES 4

Szechwan Peppercorn Vinaigrette

1 tablespoon Szechwan peppercorns

¼ cup rice vinegar

2 tablespoons soy sauce

¾ cup peanut oil

PREHEAT THE OVEN to 350°F.

TOAST THE SZECHWAN peppercorns in a pie tin in the preheated oven for 5 minutes. Remove the peppercorns from the oven and cool to room temperature. Once cooled, finely grind the peppercorns in a spice grinder or electric coffee grinder.

IN A 3-QUART stainless steel bowl, whisk together the rice vinegar, soy sauce, and peppercorns. Add the peanut oil in a slow, steady stream while whisking until incorporated. Cover the bowl with plastic wrap and set aside at room temperature until needed. ◉

Grilled Whole Fish with Sweet-and-Sour Sauce

Fritz Sonnenschmidt | Recipe Courtesy of the Weber-Stephen Products Co.

2 whole red snapper or striped bass (about 1½ pounds each), cleaned and scaled

2 tablespoons lime juice (about 1 medium lime)

½ teaspoon salt

¼ teaspoon freshly ground black pepper

½ cup dry sherry

1 cup plain dried bread crumbs

Sweet-and-Sour Sauce, recipe on page 82

6 Boston lettuce leaves (optional)

1 cup slivered ham (optional)

4 tablespoons red bell pepper strips (optional)

MAKE 3 SLASHES in each side of the fish. Sprinkle the fish with lime juice, salt, and pepper. Place the fish in a large resealable bag set in a shallow dish. Pour the sherry over the fish and marinate in the refrigerator for 1 hour, turning twice to distribute the marinade.

REMOVE THE FISH from the marinade and pat dry. Insert a rolled-up piece of aluminum foil into the belly of each fish and flatten to allow the fish to stand on its belly. Spray the fish with nonstick cooking spray. Roll the fish in the bread crumbs, pressing lightly to coat both sides with crumbs.

PLACE THE FISH supported by the foil upright on the grill's cooking grate. Grill over medium-high heat for 20 to 30 minutes, or until fish flakes when tested with a fork.

TO SERVE, place ¼ cup of the Sweet-and-Sour Sauce on a large platter. Remove the foil from the fish and place the fish on the sauce.

IF DESIRED, arrange the lettuce leaves as cups around the edge of the platter and fill each with equal amounts of slivered ham and red bell pepper strips. Serve the fish with additional Sweet-and-Sour Sauce. ◉

A different take on grilled whole fish, these are marinated, coated with breadcrumbs, grilled and served with a classic sweet-sour dipping sauce. Fritz uses aluminum foil to provide a stable base on which the fish rests while it is cooking. This method ensures even cooking and prevents the fish from sticking to the cooking grates during grilling.

SERVES 6

Sweet-and-Sour Sauce

3 tablespoons vegetable oil

1 large onion, sliced

¼ cup minced fresh ginger (about 2 ounces)

1 cup sliced sweet gherkins (about 5 ounces)

2 cups tomato juice

2 tablespoons honey

2 tablespoons cider or white vinegar

1 tablespoon reduced-sodium soy sauce

2 tablespoons quick-cooking tapioca or cornstarch

Salt and freshly ground black pepper to taste

HEAT THE OIL in large saucepan over medium-high heat. Add the onion, ginger, and gherkins and cook for 5 minutes, stirring constantly until tender. Add the tomato juice, honey, vinegar, and soy sauce; heat until the mixture comes to a boil. Add the tapioca or cornstarch and stir until the sauce is slightly thickened. Season with salt and pepper. ◉

Grilled Tuna Steak with Nectarine-Red Onion Relish

Chris Schlesinger | Reprinted from *The Thrill of the Grill*, William Morrow and Company

Nectarine-Red Onion Relish

1 red bell pepper, seeded and cut into thin strips

6 ripe but firm nectarines, peeled and cut into 8 slices each

1 medium red onion, sliced into long, thin pieces

1 teaspoon minced garlic

¼ cup red wine vinegar

¼ cup fresh orange juice

2 tablespoons lime juice (about 1 lime)

¼ cup virgin olive oil

Salt and freshly ground black pepper to taste

Four 8- to 10-ounce boneless tuna steaks, about 1-inch thick

4 tablespoons vegetable oil

Salt and freshly ground pepper (white is best) to taste

FOR THE RELISH, combine all the ingredients in a large bowl and toss them gently. This will be a slightly runny relish, as the solids and liquids mix but do not combine. Keep chilled until ready to serve. This relish will keep, covered and refrigerated, up to 2 weeks.

LIGHTLY RUB THE TUNA steaks with the vegetable oil and season with salt and pepper. Grill the tuna steaks for 4 to 5 minutes per side over medium-high heat, being careful not to overcook them. Check for doneness by bending a steak gently and peering inside it, looking for a slight translucence in the center. Remove the steaks from the grill and place them on top of the relish on serving plates. ◉

Tuna's meaty texture and flavor make it a good choice of fish for grilling. Here, Chris cooks his tuna until it's still slightly rare in the middle and offsets it with a tangy fruit salsa.

SERVES 6

Sesame-Soy Tuna with Napa Cabbage and Cracked Black Pepper Butter

Marcel Desaulniers

This dish has many colors, flavors, and textures, but they are surprisingly complementary. The recipe may seem long, but much of the preparation can be done ahead of time. Grill the tuna steaks medium-rare for a delicious, meaty mouthful.

SERVES 4

4 tablespoons rice vinegar

3 tablespoons soy sauce

2 tablespoons fresh lemon juice (about ½ lemon)

1 tablespoon granulated sugar

1 tablespoon creamy-style peanut butter

1 teaspoon minced garlic

1 cup peanut oil

½ cup safflower oil

1 tablespoon toasted sesame oil

Salt and freshly ground black pepper to taste

Four 4- to 5-ounce tuna fillets, about ¾-inch thick

¼ pound unsalted butter, softened

3 tablespoons minced shallots

3 ounces dry white wine

½ tablespoon cracked black peppercorns

1 medium carrot, peeled and cut into strips 2½-inches long and ⅛-inch wide

4 sun-dried tomatoes, packed in oil

1½ pounds napa cabbage, discolored outer leaves removed, cored, and sliced ¼-inch thick

½ tablespoon chopped fresh parsley

½ tablespoon sesame seeds, toasted

FOR THE MARINADE, whisk together, in a 5-quart stainless steel bowl, the rice vinegar, soy sauce, lemon juice, sugar, peanut butter, and garlic. Add the peanut oil, safflower oil, and sesame oil in a slow, steady stream, whisking until incorporated. Season with salt and pepper. Place the tuna steaks into the marinade, cover with plastic wrap and refrigerate for 30 minutes.

HEAT 1 TABLESPOON of the butter in a nonstick sauté pan over medium heat. When hot, add the minced shallots, season with salt and pepper and sauté for 1 minute. Add the wine and bring to a simmer; adjust the heat and simmer until the pan is almost dry, about 5 minutes. Remove the pan from the heat, transfer the mixture to a stainless steel bowl, and cool. When the mixture is cool, combine with the remaining butter and cracked black peppercorns and mix until well blended. Cover the black pepper butter with plastic wrap and set aside at room temperature until needed.

COOK THE CARROT STRIPS in boiling salted water for 1½ minutes. Drain and transfer immediately to ice water. When cool, drain thoroughly.

DRAIN THE SUN-DRIED tomatoes on paper towels, then cut them into thin strips.

HEAT THE BLACK PEPPER BUTTER and 2 tablespoons of water in a large nonstick sauté pan over high heat. When hot, add the carrots, and sauté for 1 minute. Add the cabbage, season with salt and pepper, and sauté for 1½ minutes. Add the sun-dried tomatoes, mix thoroughly, remove the pan from the heat and keep warm.

REMOVE THE TUNA from the marinade and place on a grill over medium heat. Grill for 2 minutes on each side for medium rare; cook longer for more well-done tuna.

DIVIDE THE CABBAGE-CARROT mixture among 4 dinner plates. Place a grilled tuna fillet on each portion of cabbage and garnish with chopped parsley and toasted sesame seeds. Serve immediately. ◉

Cinnamon-Grilled Salmon with Citrus and Port-Soaked Dried Fruit

Marcel Desaulniers

½ cup dried currants

½ cup raisins

½ cup plus 1 tablespoon port wine

1 tablespoon fresh orange juice

½ tablespoon cider vinegar

1 teaspoon honey

¼ teaspoon finely minced orange zest

3 tablespoons extra-virgin olive oil

2 tablespoons safflower oil

Salt and freshly ground black pepper to taste

3 tablespoons fresh lemon juice (about ¾ lemon)

Four 4- to 5-ounce skinless salmon fillets

2 teaspoons ground cinnamon

*4 medium pink grapefruit (about 14 ounces each), peeled and
   cut into ¼-inch-thick slices*

*4 large navel oranges (about 8 ounces each), peeled and
   cut into ¼-inch-thick slices*

A clean-tasting citrus vinaigrette is a nice contrast to the rich flavor of the salmon. A hint of cinnamon lends an exotic flair. The raisins and currants must soak for 12 hours, so plan ahead.

SERVES 4

COMBINE THE CURRANTS and raisins in a 1-quart stainless steel bowl. Heat ½ cup port wine in a 1½-quart saucepan over medium-high heat. When the wine begins to simmer, remove from the heat and pour over the raisins and currants. Cover the bowl with plastic wrap and set aside at room temperature for 12 hours.

continued on next page

Cinnamon-Grilled Salmon Fillet with Citrus and Port-Soaked Dried Fruit (continued)

MAKE A CITRUS VINAIGRETTE by whisking together in a 3-quart stainless steel bowl the orange juice, 1 tablespoon port wine, cider vinegar, honey, and orange zest. Add 2 tablespoons of the olive oil and the safflower oil in a slow, steady stream, whisking until incorporated. Season with salt and pepper. Cover the bowl with plastic wrap and set aside at room temperature.

SPRINKLE THE LEMON JUICE and remaining 1 tablespoon extra-virgin olive oil over the salmon fillets. Season both sides of the salmon fillets with salt, pepper, and cinnamon. Grill the salmon fillets over medium heat for 3 to 3½ minutes on each side. Keep warm.

DIVIDE AND ARRANGE the grapefruit and orange slices (alternately) in a circle on each of 4 dinner plates. Vigorously whisk the vinaigrette. Drizzle the sliced citrus fruit on each plate with 1 to 1½ tablespoons of vinaigrette. Sprinkle 2 to 3 tablespoons of the port-soaked currants and raisins over the citrus fruit. Place a portion of grilled salmon on each plate and serve immediately. ◉

Grilled Skewers of Catfish with Black-Eyed Pea Salad

Marcel Desaulniers

1½ pounds catfish fillet, cut into 1- to 1½-inch pieces

4 tablespoons peanut oil

1 tablespoon fresh lemon juice

Salt and freshly ground black pepper to taste

Black-Eyed Pea Salad, page 51

1 head curly endive, cut into 2-inch pieces, washed and dried

COMBINE THE CATFISH pieces with the peanut oil and lemon juice, season with salt and pepper and combine thoroughly. Divide the catfish into 4 portions. Thread each portion onto a skewer.

GRILL THE CATFISH skewers over medium-high heat for 6 minutes, turning occasionally to prevent burning.

REMOVE THE GRILLED CATFISH from the skewers. Serve immediately accompanied by the Black-Eyed Pea Salad. Garnish with curly endive pieces. ◉

Though most catfish available today is farmed, it is native to the rivers of the southern United States and is popular in southern-style cooking. Black eyed-peas are another staple of Dixie cuisine and are an apt companion to grilled catfish chunks.

SERVES 4

Grilled Gravlax with Grilled Caraway Potatoes, Mustard Sauce, and Dill Salsa

Fritz Sonnenschmidt

2 ounces sugar

2 ounces kosher salt

½ teaspoon ground white pepper

2½ pounds salmon fillet

2 tablespoons coarsely chopped fresh dill

Vegetable oil

Mustard Sauce, recipe on page 92

Grilled Caraway Potatoes, page 47

Dill Salsa, recipe on page 92

IN A SMALL BOWL, mix the sugar, salt, and white pepper.

PLACE THE SALMON skin–side down in a stainless steel or porcelain dish. Coat the salmon evenly on all sides with the sugar–salt mixture and sprinkle with the dill. Cover the dish with plastic wrap and refrigerate for 3 to 4 days, turning the fish daily.

REMOVE THE SALMON from the dish and rinse with cold water. Pat the fish dry with paper towels and cut into 4 portions.

BRUSH THE SALMON portions with oil and place on a grill over medium–high heat. Grill the salmon for about 2 minutes on each side.

TO SERVE, spoon a pool of Mustard Sauce in the center of 4 serving plates. Place a grilled potato on top of the sauce and top with a grilled salmon portion. Drizzle the Dill Salsa on the plate around the fish. ◉

Gravlax, a Swedish delicacy, consists of raw salmon that is cured in a mixture of salt, sugar, and fresh dill. Though usually sliced thinly and served as an appetizer, Fritz offers a new entrée version, which is grilled and presented with a duo of complementary sauces.

SERVES 4

Mustard Sauce

1 tablespoon unsalted butter

2 tablespoons chopped shallots

1 tablespoon flour

3 cups cold chicken broth

1 bay leaf

2 tablespoons Dixon's or Gulden's mustard

4 tablespoons whipped cream

Salt and freshly ground white pepper to taste

IN A SKILLET, heat the butter over medium heat. Add the shallots and sauté for about 3 minutes. Add the flour and sauté for 2 to 3 minutes over low heat. Add the chicken broth, mix well and bring to a boil over high heat. Add the bay leaf and continue to cook until the mixture is reduced by half.

STIR IN THE MUSTARD and simmer for 5 minutes. Remove the sauce from the heat and remove and discard the bay leaf; cool slightly. Fold in the whipped cream and season with salt and pepper. ◉

Dill Salsa

4 tablespoons coarsely chopped fresh dill

2 to 3 ounces olive oil

½ teaspoon sugar

½ teaspoon salt

¼ teaspoon freshly ground white pepper

1 tablespoon fresh lemon juice

PLUNGE THE DILL into a pot of rapidly boiling water for a few seconds, until the color turns vibrant green; remove and plunge into ice water.

DRAIN THE DILL, combine with the oil, sugar, salt, pepper, and lemon juice and puree in a blender. ◉

Citrus-Marinated Mahi Mahi with Fresh Herb Couscous

Marcel Desaulniers

2 tablespoons fresh orange juice

1 tablespoon fresh lemon juice

1 tablespoon dry white wine

¼ cup plus 1 tablespoon extra-virgin olive oil

¼ cup safflower oil

Salt and freshly ground black pepper to taste

Four 4- to 5-ounce boneless and skinless mahi mahi fillets

Fresh Herb Couscous, page 41

1 lemon, peeled and sectioned for garnish

1 tablespoon chopped fresh dill for garnish

MAKE A MARINADE by whisking together in a 3-quart stainless steel bowl the orange juice, lemon juice, and wine. Add ¼ cup olive oil and the safflower oil in a slow, steady stream while whisking until incorporated. Season with salt and pepper.

LIGHTLY SEASON EACH SIDE of the mahi mahi fillets with salt and pepper. Place the fillets into the citrus marinade, cover with plastic wrap and refrigerate for 30 to 45 minutes.

REMOVE THE FILLETS from the marinade and grill over medium heat until done, about 4½ minutes on each side. Serve the grilled mahi mahi with the Fresh Herb Couscous, and garnish with lemon sections and chopped dill. ◉

A team of citrus juices with fresh herbs and fruity olive oil are a simple way to enliven grilled fish fillets. The dish is quick to prepare, requiring only a short marinating before grilling.

SERVES 4

Cedar Plank Grilled Salmon with Ginger Sauce and Chili Oil

Fritz Sonnenschmidt

1 teaspoon kosher salt

¼ teaspoon freshly ground white pepper

Four 8-ounce boneless, skinless salmon steaks

2 tablespoons olive oil

*2 untreated cedar shingles, approximately 12 inches long and
   4 to 5 inches wide*

Ginger Sauce, follows

Chili Oil, follows

Grilled scallions for garnish

IN A SMALL BOWL or cup, combine the salt and white pepper.

BRUSH THE SALMON steaks with the oil and sprinkle with the salt mixture on both sides.

SOAK THE CEDAR PLANKS in ice water for about 15 minutes. Place the soaked shingles on a grill over high heat. Close the grill cover and let shingles "cook" for 2 to 3 minutes, until one side has browned slightly.

TURN THE SHINGLES OVER and place a salmon fillet on the browned side of each shingle. Grill the salmon over medium heat for 6 to 7 minutes, turning once, until the salmon is firm but not dry.

SPOON A POOL of ginger sauce onto each of 4 warm serving plates. Place the grilled salmon on top of the sauce. Drizzle the chili oil around the salmon on the plate and garnish with grilled scallions. ◉

"Planking" fish, or grilling fish directly on thin pieces of wood, infuses it with intense wood-smoke flavor. This method of cooking, borrowed from the American Indians, is popular in the Pacific Northwest, where the salmon run wild in the rivers.

SERVES 4

Ginger Sauce

2 tablespoons butter

3 ounces fresh ginger, peeled and chopped

2 ounces chopped onions

¼ cup flour

2 cups chicken broth

2 cups fat-free condensed milk

3 tablespoons whipped cream

Salt and freshly ground white pepper to taste

IN A SKILLET, heat the butter over medium heat. Add the ginger and onions and sauté for about 3 minutes, until softened. Add the flour and sauté for 2 minutes. Add the chicken broth and bring to a boil. Cook until the mixture is reduced by half.

ADD THE CONDENSED MILK and cook until the mixture is reduced by half.

STRAIN THE SAUCE through a fine sieve; cool slightly. Fold in the whipped cream and season with salt and pepper. ◉

Chili Oil

3 ounces walnut oil

1 teaspoon chili powder

¼ teaspoon ground cinnamon

IN A SMALL SAUCEPAN, combine all the ingredients and heat until the mixture reaches 140°F. Cool and strain. Transfer the chili oil to a tightly capped bottle and refrigerate until ready to use. Bring to room temperature before using. ◉

Grilled Sea Scallops with Zucchini and Country Ham

Marcel Desaulniers

Most of the country ham available comes from the southern states. You may have to order it by mail if you can't find it at a local specialty food store. It's worth the trouble to find it, though. Its salt-cured flavor goes nicely with the mild, meaty flavor of scallops. Ask your fishmonger for scallops that are just-caught and that are "dry," or untreated with water or chemicals.

SERVES 4

2 pounds zucchini, lightly peeled

1 ½ pounds sea scallops, side muscle removed

3 tablespoons safflower oil

Salt and ground cayenne pepper to taste

4 tablespoons butter

¼ pound country ham, cut into strips 1 ¼-inches long and ⅛-inch thick

½ tablespoon chopped fresh dill

USING A MANDOLINE, cut the zucchini into long, thin, spaghetti–like strands the length of the zucchini and about ⅛–inch wide. Refrigerate until needed.

PREHEAT THE OVEN to 225°F.

IN A BOWL, toss the sea scallops with the safflower oil and lightly season with salt and cayenne pepper. Divide the scallops into 4 portions and thread each portion onto a skewer.

GRILL THE SCALLOPS over medium heat for 4 minutes, turning occasionally to prevent burning. Transfer the skewers to a nonstick baking sheet and hold in the preheated oven while cooking the zucchini.

MELT THE BUTTER in a large nonstick sauté pan over medium–high heat. When hot, place the zucchini strips in the pan. Lightly season with salt and cayenne pepper and sauté until hot, about 5 minutes. Add the country ham and chopped dill and toss to combine.

DIVIDE THE ZUCCHINI strips among 4 soup/pasta plates. Remove the scallops from the skewers and place in the center of each portion of zucchini. ◉

Linguine with Grilled Shrimp and Black Olives

Chris Schlesinger | Reprinted from *License to Grill*, William Morrow and Company

24 medium shrimp (about 1½ pounds), peeled and deveined

Salt and freshly ground black pepper to taste

12 ounces linguine or other dried pasta

6 tablespoons extra-virgin olive oil

4 cloves garlic, sliced lengthwise as thinly as possible

5 vine-ripened tomatoes, cored and roughly chopped

¾ cup brine-cured black olives, pitted and roughly chopped

¾ cup chopped fresh basil

¼ cup freshly grated hard Italian cheese, such as Parmesan or Asiago

SPRINKLE THE SHRIMP generously with salt and pepper and thread them onto skewers. Grill the shrimp over medium–high heat for 3 to 4 minutes per side. To check for doneness: Cut into one of the shrimp and check to be sure it is opaque all the way through. Remove the shrimp from grill, remove from the skewers, and chop each shrimp into 3 or 4 pieces. Set aside.

IN A LARGE POT, bring about 4 quarts of salted water to a rapid boil over high heat. Add the pasta, return to a boil, and cook until just tender but not mushy, 8 to 10 minutes. Drain and place in a large bowl.

WHILE THE PASTA is cooking, heat the olive oil in a small sauté pan over medium heat until hot but not smoking. Add the garlic and cook, stirring frequently, until it just starts to brown, 2 to 3 minutes. Remove from the heat.

POUR THE OIL and garlic over the pasta. Add the tomatoes, olives, chopped shrimp, and the basil, and toss together. Adjust the seasonings, top with the grated cheese, and serve. ◉

Mediterranean flavors invigorate a simple dish of linguine and shrimp. According to Chris, it's a good recipe to keep in mind when unexpected guests stop by because it can be put together at the last minute. Even without the shrimp, this is a marvelous, easy dish.

SERVES 4 AS ENTRéE, 6 TO 8 AS APPETIZER

Mixed Grill of Seafood with Fresh Herb Sauce and Ricotta Soufflés

Fritz Sonnenschmidt

Ask your fishmonger to cut the fish into medallions—small coin-shaped pieces of boneless fish. The fish and shrimp will cook very quickly on the grill. Be sure to have the rest of the recipe's elements ready before grilling the seafood.

SERVES 4

¼ cup balsamic vinegar

2 tablespoons sesame oil

1 teaspoon honey

1 tablespoon hoisin sauce

1 medium zucchini, cut into 4 to 8 pieces

1 red bell pepper, seeded and cut into 4 wedges

8 asparagus spears, tough ends trimmed, cut in half

Four 2-ounce medallions monkfish or red snapper

4 large shrimp, peeled and deveined

Four 2-ounce medallions salmon

Salt and freshly ground black pepper to taste

Vegetable oil

Fresh Herb Sauce, follows

Ricotta Soufflés, page 43

4 sprigs fresh dill for garnish

IN A LARGE SHALLOW DISH, combine the balsamic vinegar, sesame oil, honey and hoisin sauce. Add the zucchini, red pepper and asparagus spears and toss to coat well. Cover the dish and marinate the vegetables for 1 hour.

REMOVE THE VEGETABLES from the marinade and place on the grill over high heat. Cook for 3 to 4 minutes per side, until tender–crisp. As the vegetables are done, remove them from the grill and keep warm.

SEASON THE MONKFISH (or snapper), shrimp and salmon with salt and pepper and brush with vegetable oil. Place the fish and shrimp on the grill over high heat and cook for 2 minutes on each side.

TO SERVE, drizzle the Fresh Herb Sauce on each of four dinner plates. Arrange the fish, shrimp, vegetables and Ricotta Soufflés on top of the sauce and garnish with dill sprigs. Serve immediately. ◉

Fresh Herb Sauce

3 tablespoons unsalted butter

4 shallots, minced

1 cup dry white wine

½ cup chicken broth

¼ cup heavy cream

1 small bay leaf

6 black peppercorns, crushed

1 tablespoon chopped fresh parsley

1 tablespoon chopped fresh chervil

1 tablespoon chopped fresh dill

Salt and freshly ground black pepper to taste

IN A SKILLET over medium heat, melt the butter. Add the shallots and sauté for 2 minutes. Add the wine, chicken broth, cream, bay leaf and peppercorns and bring to a boil over high heat. Cook until the mixture is reduced by half.

STRAIN THE MIXTURE through a sieve. Stir in the herbs and season with salt and pepper to taste. ◉

Meat

Grilled Medallions of Veal with Apples, Pears, and Nutmeg Cream

Marcel Desaulniers

1 cup heavy cream

1 teaspoon freshly grated nutmeg

1 tablespoon fresh lemon juice

2 Granny Smith apples, unpeeled

1 large pear, unpeeled

1 pound well-trimmed boneless veal loin, cut into 16 ¼-inch-thick medallions

2 tablespoons extra-virgin olive oil

Salt and freshly ground black pepper to taste

Hot cooked wild rice

HEAT THE HEAVY CREAM and grated nutmeg in a small saucepan over medium heat. Adjust the heat so that the cream barely simmers.

ACIDULATE 4 CUPS of water with the lemon juice in a 3-quart stainless steel bowl. Core and quarter the unpeeled apples and pear. Slice the apples and pear widthwise into the acidulated water. Drain the sliced apples and pear in a colander and rinse under cold running water. Shake dry.

TRANSFER THE APPLES and pear to a large nonstick sauté pan. Add the hot nutmeg cream. Keep hot while grilling the veal.

LIGHTLY COAT THE VEAL medallions with olive oil and season with salt and pepper. Quickly sear the medallions on the grill over medium–high heat. Serve the veal on a bed of wild rice surrounded by the apples, pears, and nutmeg cream. ◉

Reserve this dish for a holiday dinner party on a cold winter night. The elegant spice-infused cream sauce is a lovely companion to wild rice, winter fruits and rounds of grilled veal.

SERVES 4

Grilled Big Black-and-Blue Steak for Two

Chris Schlesinger | Reprinted from *The Thrill of the Grill*, William Morrow and Company

Definitely buy the best-quality meat you can find, as it is nearly the only ingredient in this recipe. Don't be afraid to blacken the surface of the steak completely over the coals. The hot, smoky crust will be a good foil to the cool, luscious meat on the inside. Serve it with the classic accompaniments— a baked potato and a tossed green salad.

SERVES 2

One giant 1½-inch-thick steak (choose one of the following)
  One 2-pound boneless Delmonico or
  One 2½-pound bone-in Delmonico or
  One 2½-pound porterhouse

¼ cup olive oil

Kosher salt and freshly cracked black pepper to taste

ALLOW THE STEAK to come to room temperature, then rub it with the oil and salt and pepper to taste.

OVER A MEDIUM-HOT FIRE, grill the steak until the exterior is very brown, almost black, and very crusty, about 8 to 9 minutes per side. Some flare-ups might occur. If they do, remove the steak from the grill using long tongs, allow the fire to calm down, and place the steak back on the grill. To check for doneness, nick the meat on one side and look at the color. It will appear slightly rarer than it will actually be after resting.

REMOVE THE STEAK from the fire, allow it to rest 5 minutes, and serve. ◐

Grilled Mushroom-Stuffed Beef Tenderloin with Trellis Steak Sauce

Marcel Desaulniers

Trellis Steak Sauce

1 pound plus 1 tablespoon unsalted butter, softened

6 tablespoons minced shallots

Salt and freshly ground black pepper to taste

¼ cup sour mash whiskey

6 tablespoons sauce Robert (see Note)

2 teaspoons extra-virgin olive oil

1 cup thinly sliced red onions

Salt and freshly ground black pepper to taste

¼ cup dry white wine

¼ pound shiitake mushrooms, stemmed and thinly sliced

1 teaspoon chopped fresh herbs

Four 4-ounce beef tenderloin steaks, about 1-inch thick

MAKE THE TRELLIS STEAK SAUCE: Heat 1 tablespoon butter in a small nonstick sauté pan over medium heat. When the butter is hot, add the minced shallots, season very lightly with salt and pepper, and sauté for 1 minute. Add the sour mash whiskey and bring to a simmer, reduce the heat, and simmer until the pan is almost dry, about 8 minutes. Remove the pan from the heat, and allow to cool.

PLACE THE REMAINING 1 pound softened butter in the bowl of a food processor fitted with the metal blade. Add the cooled shallot and whiskey mixture, and the sauce Robert. Process the mixture until smooth and well combined. Using a rubber spatula, remove the sauce from the processor and place in a stainless steel bowl. Cover the steak sauce with plastic wrap, and set aside at room temperature until ready to use.

continued on next page

A large quantity of butter makes Marcel's signature Trellis Steak Sauce ultra-smooth. It's a fitting companion to an elegant stuffed beef tenderloin for a special occasion dinner.

SERVES 4

Grilled Mushroom-Stuffed Beef Tenderloin
with Trellis Steak Sauce (continued)

HEAT THE OLIVE OIL in a medium nonstick sauté pan over medium-high heat. When the oil is hot, add the sliced red onions, then season with salt and pepper and cook, stirring frequently, for 10 minutes until the onions are well-browned. Add the wine and cook for 30 seconds. Add the shiitake mushrooms and chopped herbs and cook for 6 minutes, stirring frequently. Transfer the mixture to a pie plate and place uncovered in the refrigerator to cool.

WHILE THE MIXTURE is cooling, prepare the steaks for stuffing. Use a thin-bladed sharp knife to make a 1-inch-wide and 1½-inch-deep horizontal incision into the side of each steak. Use an index finger to enlarge the pocket without actually poking through the sides of the steak. Stuff an equal amount (about 1 heaping tablespoon) of the chilled mushroom and herb mixture into each steak pocket. Season both sides of each steak with salt and freshly ground black pepper.

GRILL THE STEAKS over medium-high heat for 2½ minutes on each side for rare to medium-rare; 3 minutes on each side for medium-rare to medium; 4 minutes on each side for a solid medium; and about 5 minutes on each side for well-done. Serve the steaks with the Trellis Steak Sauce.

NOTE: Sauce Robert is available in six-ounce bottles at most gourmet/fancy food stores. ◉

Charred Tenderloin of Beef with Summer Vegetable Ratatouille

Marcel Desaulniers

One 1-pound piece beef tenderloin, well-trimmed

2 tablespoons extra-virgin olive oil

Salt to taste

3 tablespoons freshly cracked black peppercorns

Summer Vegetable Ratatouille, page 32

PLACE THE BEEF TENDERLOIN in a pie tin or similar size shallow dish. Coat the meat evenly with the olive oil. Season the tenderloin with salt, then sprinkle the cracked black peppercorns onto the meat, covering as much of the surface area as possible. Use your hands to press the peppercorns into the meat.

PLACE THE TENDERLOIN on an extremely hot grill and char evenly by turning frequently for 3 to 4 minutes for rare meat; cook longer for meat that's more well done. Remove the tenderloin from the grill and transfer to a dish or plate large enough to hold it. Refrigerate the tenderloin for 1½ to 2 hours, until thoroughly chilled.

PLACE THE TENDERLOIN on a cutting board and use a very sharp slicer to cut the meat into very thin slices (the meat should yield 16 to 20 slices). Serve with the Summer Vegetable Ratatouille. ◉

For this dish, a peppercorn-encrusted tenderloin is quickly seared on an extremely hot grill. After chilling completely, the steak is sliced very thinly and served cold. This dish is a perfect choice to serve on a hot summer day because all of the preparation can be done in advance.

SERVES 4

Jerking is a cooking preparation common to the island of Jamaica. Usually very spicy, a jerk seasoning blend consists of herbs, spices, and chiles, which are finely ground and rubbed onto the surface of meats and poultry before cooking. For an authentic presentation, pull the pork into shreds with your fingers.

SERVES 10 TO 12

Grilled Jerked Pork with Pineapple Chutney

Fritz Sonnenschmidt | Recipe Courtesy of the Weber-Stephen Products Co.

1 medium-sized yellow onion, minced

6 scallions with ½-inch green tops, trimmed and finely chopped

3 cloves garlic, minced

2 red finger chile peppers, seeded, deveined, and finely chopped

1 teaspoon finely chopped fresh thyme

1 teaspoon cider or distilled white vinegar

1 teaspoon ground allspice

1 teaspoon packed brown sugar

½ teaspoon ground cinnamon

½ teaspoon ground nutmeg

½ teaspoon ground black pepper

½ teaspoon salt

¼ cup olive oil

One 4-pound boneless pork loin or pork shoulder roast (Boston butt)

Pineapple Chutney, follows

IN A SMALL BOWL, mix together the onion, scallions, garlic, chile peppers, and thyme. Add the vinegar, allspice, brown sugar, cinnamon, nutmeg, pepper, and salt; mix well. Add the olive oil and mix well.

PLACE THE PORK ROAST in large resealable plastic bag. Pour the marinade over the roast, rubbing and pressing it into the surface of the meat. Close the bag. Marinate the pork in the refrigerator for 6 to 8 hours or overnight, turning the bag occasionally to distribute the marinade.

REMOVE THE ROAST from the marinade. Place the roast in the center of the cooking grate on a medium–hot grill. Grill for 2½ to 3 hours for well–done (170°F), or until tender.

REMOVE THE PORK from the grill and let stand, covered, for 5 minutes. Shred or cut the pork into 1–inch slivers. Serve with Pineapple Chutney. ◉

Pineapple Chutney

One 20-ounce can crushed pineapple

1 cup white balsamic vinegar

1 cup packed brown sugar

1 small red onion, minced

1 tablespoon minced fresh ginger

1 red finger chile pepper, seeded, deveined, and minced

IN A 2-QUART SAUCEPAN, combine the pineapple, vinegar, brown sugar, red onion, ginger, and chile pepper.

BRING THE MIXTURE to a boil over high heat. Reduce the heat to low and simmer uncovered for about 30 to 40 minutes. Cool.

STORE THE SAUCE covered in the refrigerator until ready to use, or up to 10 days. ◉

Grilled Pork Chops and Peaches with Molasses-Rum Barbecue Sauce

Chris Schlesinger | Reprinted from *License to Grill*, William Morrow and Company

Four 14- to 16-ounce double-thick rib or loin pork chops

2 tablespoons vegetable oil

Salt and freshly ground black pepper to taste

Molasses-Rum Barbecue Sauce

2 tablespoons vegetable oil

1 large yellow onion, diced medium

2 tablespoons minced fresh ginger

2 tablespoons minced garlic

1 cup rum

½ cup red wine vinegar

1 cup ketchup

½ cup molasses

¼ cup lightly packed brown sugar

1 tablespoon ground allspice

Pinch of ground mace

Salt and freshly ground black pepper to taste

4 ripe peaches, halved and pitted

BUILD A SMALL CHARCOAL FIRE in one side of the grill, using enough charcoal to fill a shoebox.

RUB THE CHOPS lightly with the oil, sprinkle with salt and pepper to taste, and set aside while you begin the sauce.

continued on next page

You will likely need to visit a butcher shop to get pork chops this thick. Chris prefers the rib chops because they are a little neater-looking than the loin chops. Wait until the last minute to brush with the sauce to get a nice caramelized coating without burning. The peaches go well with other grilled meats, too.

SERVES 4

Grilled Pork Chops and Peaches with
Molasses-Rum Barbecue Sauce (continued)

MAKE THE SAUCE: In a small saucepan over medium heat, heat the oil until hot but not smoking. Add the onion and sauté, stirring occasionally, until transparent, 5 to 7 minutes. Add the ginger and garlic and sauté, stirring, for 1 minute. Add the rum, vinegar, ketchup, molasses, sugar, allspice, and mace and bring just to a boil. Reduce the heat to low and simmer gently for 20 minutes, then remove from the heat, season to taste, and set aside.

ONCE THE SAUCE is at the final simmering stage, place the chops on the grill directly over a hot fire and cook for 3 to 4 minutes per side to sear them well. When they are nicely seared, move the chops to the side of the grill with no fire and let them cook slowly for about 10 minutes per side. To check for doneness: Cut into one chop to make sure it is cooked through and slightly pink at the center.

SHORTLY BEFORE THE CHOPS are done, place the peaches on the grill just at the edge of the fire, cut-side down, and grill for 3 to 4 minutes on each side, or until they are seared and tender.

DURING THE LAST MINUTE of cooking, brush both the chops and peaches with the sauce. Allow to cook for 1 minute more, then remove from the grill and serve with the extra sauce on the side. ◉

Grilled Madras Lamb Chops with Oven-Roasted Fruit

Marcel Desaulniers

1 medium pineapple (about 2 to 2½ pounds)

4 small plums (about 2 ounces each)

2 small peaches (about 2 ounces each)

1 teaspoon curry powder

1 teaspoon dry mustard

¼ teaspoon cracked black pepper

¼ teaspoon ground cardamom

¼ teaspoon ground cayenne pepper

¼ teaspoon ground cumin

¼ teaspoon salt

⅛ teaspoon ground allspice

Four 8-ounce lamb chops

PREHEAT THE OVEN to 225°F. Line 2 baking sheets with parchment paper.

PEEL, QUARTER, AND CORE the pineapple. Cut each cored quarter widthwise into ¾-inch-thick pieces. Place the pineapple pieces, evenly spaced, onto one of the parchment–lined baking sheets. Set aside.

continued on next page

This dish has flavors reminiscent of the Indian city of Madras, where the food is fiery hot. The fruits, roasted slowly in the oven, resemble chutney, the perfect condiment for Indian-spiced food.

SERVES 4

Grilled Madras Lamb Chops with Oven-Roasted Fruit (continued)

WASH, THEN PIT, the plums and peaches. Cut each plum half into 2 pieces and each peach half into 3 pieces. Place the plum and peach pieces, cut-side up and evenly spaced, onto a parchment-lined baking sheet. Place the baking sheets on the top and center racks of the preheated oven and roast the fruit for 1½ hours, rotating the sheets from top to center halfway through the roasting time (at that time also turn each sheet 180 degrees).

REMOVE THE FRUIT from the oven and transfer to a 5-quart stainless steel bowl. Using a rubber spatula, gently combine the fruit. Cover the bowl with aluminum foil and set aside while preparing the lamb chops.

THOROUGHLY COMBINE the spices in a 5-quart stainless steel bowl. Add the lamb chops and coat evenly and completely with the spices.

GRILL THE LAMB CHOPS over medium heat for 3 to 4 minutes on each side for rare to medium-rare, and longer if you prefer more well-done meat. Serve the lamb chops with the warm oven-roasted fruit. ◉

Horseradish-Crusted Lamb Cutlets with Maple-Brandy Sauce

Fritz Sonnenschmidt

Ask your butcher to cut the lamb into cutlets: thin boneless pieces of meat from the leg or rib section of the lamb. Fresh horseradish appears as a long, brown root. Look for it in a specialty food store in the produce section. To prepare the horseradish, pare the brown fibrous peel with a vegetable peeler. Grate the white flesh by hand on a box grater or in a food processor. A word of caution: horseradish is very pungent. It will affect your eyes and nose intensely.

SERVES 6

1 cup freshly grated horseradish

2 tablespoons ground cumin

2 tablespoons finely chopped garlic

1 tablespoon paprika

1 teaspoon freshly ground black pepper

1 teaspoon crushed pink peppercorns

2 tablespoons kosher salt

Twelve 4-ounce lamb cutlets

Maple Brandy Sauce, follows

IN A MORTAR, combine the horseradish, cumin, garlic, paprika, pepper, pepper-corns and salt. With a pestle, rub the ingredients until a paste is formed.

LIGHTLY RUB the horseradish paste into the lamb cutlets.

LIGHTLY SPRAY the coated lamb cutlets with nonstick cooking spray and grill over medium-high heat for 2 to 3 minutes per side.

SERVE THE LAMB cutlets with Maple-Brandy Sauce. ◉

Maple-Brandy Sauce

2 tablespoons olive oil

1 cup finely chopped Vidalia or other sweet onions

2 tablespoons finely minced garlic

1 cup tomato ketchup

½ cup maple syrup

½ cup balsamic vinegar

¾ cup brandy

Salt and freshly ground black pepper to taste

IN A SKILLET, heat the oil over medium heat. Add the onions and garlic and sauté for about 3 minutes, until softened.

ADD THE KETCHUP, maple syrup, balsamic vinegar, and brandy. Simmer the mixture over low heat for 20 to 25 minutes. Season with salt and pepper. ◉

Caramelized Onion and Lamb Burgers with Shiitake Mushroom Chutney

Marcel Desaulniers

1 pound fresh shiitake mushrooms

1 small red onion, cut into ½-inch pieces

1 small green bell pepper, seeded, cut into ½-inch pieces

1 small carrot, peeled, cut into ½-inch pieces

1 small stalk celery, cut into ½-inch pieces

1 Anaheim chile, seeded, cut into ½-inch pieces

½ cup tightly packed light brown sugar

¼ cup granulated sugar

¼ cup water

¼ cup cider vinegar

¼ cup sherry vinegar

½ teaspoon cracked black peppercorns

1 ½ teaspoons chopped fresh thyme

Salt and freshly ground black pepper to taste

1 tablespoon safflower oil

1 medium onion (about 6 ounces), peeled, thinly sliced

1 pound ground lamb meat from shoulder or leg

4 burger buns, cut in half

REMOVE THE STEMS from the mushrooms. Slice the mushroom caps (set aside until needed) and finely chop the stems. Place the chopped stems, red onion, green pepper, carrot, celery, and Anaheim chile in a food processor fitted with the metal blade. Pulse for 30 to 40 seconds until finely chopped.

continued on next page

Surprise the guests at your next barbecue by serving them these intriguing burgers made with earthy lamb and sweet caramelized onions. A unique shiitake mushroom chutney is an interesting way to top them off.

SERVES 4

Caramelized Onion and Lamb Burgers with Shiitake Mushroom Chutney (continued)

IN A 2-QUART stainless steel saucepan, heat the chopped mushroom mixture with both sugars, water, both vinegars, and the black peppercorns over medium-high heat. Bring the mixture to a boil then lower the heat and simmer for 30 minutes, stirring frequently. Remove the pan from the heat, add the sliced mushrooms and stir to combine.

TRANSFER THE MUSHROOM mixture to a stainless steel bowl. Add ½ teaspoon of the chopped thyme. Season with salt and pepper. Cool the chutney in an ice-water bath until cold. Cover with plastic wrap and refrigerate for 12 hours before serving.

HEAT THE SAFFLOWER OIL in a medium nonstick sauté pan over medium heat. When the oil is hot, add the sliced onion and season lightly with salt and pepper. Cook the onion, stirring as necessary to prevent sticking and burning, for 20 minutes, until golden brown. Remove the onion from the heat, add the remaining teaspoon chopped thyme, and stir to combine. Transfer to a dinner plate and place uncovered in the refrigerator to cool.

IN A 5-QUART stainless steel bowl, gently but thoroughly combine the ground lamb and the chilled caramelized onion and thyme mixture. Gently form the meat mixture into four 4-ounce, 1-inch-thick burgers. Season the burgers with salt and pepper.

GRILL THE BURGERS over medium heat for 3 minutes per side for medium rare; cook longer for more well-done burgers. Remove the burgers from the grill.

TOAST THE BUNS, cut-side down, on the grill until golden brown, about 30 seconds. Serve the burgers on the toasted buns accompanied by the mushroom chutney. ◉

Italian Sausage and Portobello "Pizza"

Fritz Sonnenschmidt

6 large portobello mushrooms, about 5 inches in diameter

6 tablespoons olive oil

Salt and freshly ground black pepper to taste

4 Italian sausages

1½ cups Italian-style tomato sauce

1½ cups shredded mozzarella cheese

6 fresh basil leaves for garnish

PREHEAT THE GRILL to medium heat.

REMOVE THE STEMS from the mushrooms and slice the stems thinly. With a spoon, scrape the "gills" from the underside of the mushroom caps; discard the gills. Brush the mushrooms with oil and season with salt and pepper.

GRILL THE ITALIAN SAUSAGE until cooked through; cool and slice thinly.

TOP THE MUSHROOM caps with the tomato sauce. Sprinkle with the sliced mushroom stems and sliced Italian sausage, and top with the cheese.

PLACE THE MUSHROOM caps on the grill and cook for 10 to 12 minutes, until the mushrooms are cooked and the cheese is melted.

REMOVE THE MUSHROOM caps from the grill and garnish with basil leaves. ◉

Impress your friends by serving them "exotic" portobello mushrooms, which are actually mature versions of brown or cremini mushrooms. The mushroom caps are solid enough to simulate pizza crust. Here, they are topped with Italian sausage, mozzarella cheese and fresh basil leaves. To speed up the cooking time, you can pregrill the mushrooms for about 5 minutes.

SERVES 6

Index

Permissions

From *Big Flavors of the Hot Sun—Hot Recipes and Cool Tips from the Spice Zone* by Chris Schlesinger and John Willoughby (William Morrow and Company, 1994) ©1994 by Chris Schlesinger and John Willoughby: Grilled Banana Splits

From *License to Grill* by Chris Schlesinger and John Willoughby (William Morrow and Company, 1997) ©1997 by Chris Schlesinger and John Willoughby: All Purpose Ash-Roasted Garlic; Barbecued Oysters (Clams) in their Shells; Basic Grilled Whole Fish; Eggplant and Tomato Hobo Pack with Lemon and Garlic; Charcoal-Grilled Pork Chops with Grilled Peaches and Molasses-Rum Barbecue Sauce; Grilled Asparagus with Garlic Mayonnaise or Simple Vinaigrette; Grilled Bananas and Pineapple with Rum-Molasses Glaze; Grilled Bread Salad with Grilled Figs; Grilled Chicken and Eggplant with North African Flavors; Grilled Chicken and Mango Salad; Grilled Eggplant Rounds with Sweet Chile Sauce; Grilled Potatoes with Yogurt-Parsley Sauce; Grilled Shrimp and Black Bean Salad with Papaya-Chile Dressing; Grilled Spicy New Potato Salad; Linguine with Grilled Shrimp and Black Olives; Orange-Sweet Potato Hobo Pack; Peach and Chicken Skewers with Middle Eastern Shake and Simple Raisin Sauce

From *The Thrill of the Grill* by Chris Schlesinger and John Willoughby (William Morrow and Company, 1990) ©1990 by Chris Schlesinger and John Willoughby: Chilled Spinach with Soy and Ginger; Grilled Big Black-and-Blue Steak for Two; Grilled Chicken Thighs with Peach, Black Olive, and Red Onion Relish; Grilled Peaches with Blue Cheese and Sweet Balsamic Glaze; Grilled Tuna Steak with Nectarine-Red Onion Relish; Seared Sirloin, Sushi-Style

The following recipes are courtesy of

Marcel Desaulniers: Charred Tenderloin of Beef with Summer Vegetable Ratatouille; Cinnamon-Grilled Salmon with Citrus Fruit and Port-Soaked Raisins and Currants; Citrus-Marinated Mahi Mahi with Fresh Herb Couscous; Grilled Caramelized Onion and Lamb Burgers with Shiitake Mushroom Chutney; Grilled Curry-Scented Shrimp with Curried Brown Rice and Grilled Red Onions; Grilled Madras Lamb Chops with Oven-Roasted Fruit; Grilled Mandarin Duck Breasts with Sesame Stir-Fried Vegetables; Grilled Medallions of Veal with Apples, Pears, and Nutmeg Cream; Grilled Mushroom-Stuffed Beef Tenderloin with Trellis Steak Sauce; Grilled Quail with Peppered Honey Peaches; Grilled Sea Scallops with Zucchini and Country Ham; Grilled Sesame-Soy Tuna with Napa Cabbage and Cracked Black Pepper Butter; Grilled Skewers of Catfish with Black-Eyed Pea Salad; Grilled Spicy Chicken Legs with Garden Slaw; Honey-Charred Duck Breasts with Red Potato Salad; Mustard-Grilled Chicken with Tomatoes, Corn, and Grits Cakes

Fritz Sonnenschmidt: Cedar Plank Grilled Salmon with Ginger Sauce and Chili Oil; Grilled Chicken Legs in Buttermilk with Grilled Caraway Potatoes and Grilled Red Cabbage; Grilled Duck, Peking Style, with Grilled Romaine Lettuce; Grilled Garlic; Grilled Fruit Medley; Grilled Gravlax with Grilled Caraway Potatoes, Mustard Sauce and Dill Salsa; Grilled Hungarian Peppers; Grilled Omelet Soufflé; Horseradish-Crusted Lamb Cutlets with Maple-Brandy Sauce; Italian Sausage and Portobello "Pizza;" Mixed Grill of Seafood with Fresh Herb Sauce and Ricotta Soufflés; Zucchini Gratin

The Weber-Stephen Products, Co. (www.weberbbq.com): Bananas Calypso; Grilled Chicken Wings; Grilled Eggplant in Mustard-Miso Sauce; Grilled Jerked Pork with Pineapple Chutney; Grilled Sweet Potato Coins; Grilled Whole Fish with Sweet-and-Sour Sauce; Tea-Smoked Duck with Spicy Eggplant in Garlic Sauce

Acknowlegments

Every maestro knows that great performance depends on talent and great tools. The Weber Stephen Products Co.'s grills are such tools. Weber, who first invented the kettle grill in the 50's, when not much was known about grilling, is a visionary company whose products have introduced millions of people to the joys of outdoor cooking. We feel honored to have their support for this project and are especially grateful to Mike Kempster, Sr., for his countless contributions and tireless support. He has been our guide and inspiration in producing this series.

The success of the series is in no small measure due to the exquisite setting so generously provided by Beaulieu Vineyards' Rutherford House in Napa Valley. It is an inspirational spot, which has not only produced some of the world's finest wines, but also represents an incomparable setting for any grilled meal. We are especially grateful to Anne Howle and her staff for having been exceptionally gracious hosts.

Anne and her staff made us feel at home, as if it is normal to have a video crew invade their offices, trample their lawns while setting up equipment and take over their kitchen for nearly two weeks. Finally we want to express our gratitude to Priscilla Felton and Beaulieu Vineyards for their tremendous support of the *Grilling Maestros* series.

Many viewers are calling to inquire about the attractive plates and serving pieces they have seen on the shows. Our thanks go to Signature Housewares, Le Creuset and Fioriware for having supplied us with such beautiful and remarkable tabletop pieces. We were most fortunate to have Catskill Craftsmen out of Stamford, New York provide us with unique wooden cutting boards and wooden prep tables for our kitchen set. A special thanks must also go to all of our other supporters, including Petaluma Poultry, Mango Imports, Lancaster Glass and Chicago Metallic.
—Marjorie Poore and Alec Fatalevich

Grilling Maestros © 1999 by Marjorie Poore Productions
Photography by Alec Fatalevich
Design: Kari Perin, Perin+Perin
Editing: Jennifer Newens
Production: Kristen Wurz

ISBN 0-9651095-5-0
Printed in Hong Kong through Global Interprint, Santa Rosa, California

10 9 8 7 6 5 4 3 2 1

MPP Books, 363 14th Avenue, San Francisco, CA 94118
Distributed by Bristol Publishing Enterprises, Inc.